AF429168

Default Settings

Jonathan Blow

Published by Jonathan Blow, 2024.

While every precaution has been taken in the preparation of this book, the publisher assumes no responsibility for errors or omissions, or for damages resulting from the use of the information contained herein.

DEFAULT SETTINGS

First edition. May 3, 2024.

Copyright © 2024 Jonathan Blow.

ISBN: 979-8224468935

Written by Jonathan Blow.

Default Setting
Jonathan Blow
Parts of my life

Introduction

I'm in prison!

Every morning I wake up in shock to the prison doors being unlocked.

I stare at the concrete walls, the concrete floor and the barred windows giving a glimpse of daylight, thinking - how did I end up here?

This is what my story is about, about how I ended up in prison, about my default setting.

Default setting is the setting we are born with, the setting that God provides us with no matter who your parents are, or where on earth they come from.

Much like the majority of electronic gadgets we buy.

For an example, a cellphone comes with a factory default setting.

A setting that is provided by it's maker to ensure the phone works to a set minimum standard.

You don't accept lower than the default setting.

If something is wrong with the phone, you simply return it.

But .... you can't return a human!!!

Once you have your new phone, it's up to you to change the settings to your liking.

You are the controller of the phone - just like a parent is the controller of a new born baby.

So you go ahead and add applications, adjust wallpapers and colors, change battery life settings, adjust brightness and font sizes (make it bigger for people who can't see very well, like me).

You eventually end up with a completely different phone to the one you brought (or have stolen like many of my cell mates have done).

"Don't be fooled!

Bad companions ruin good character!"

Corinthians 15:33

What caused the change to the phone?

- Outside influences - those companies that create the apps;

- Experiences - when using the phone you discover that the irritating screen saver is coming on too soon. So you adjust it to appear after 10 minutes instead;

- Learnings - you learn from other people and from the phone's help guide/instruction manual, on better settings to use on your phone;

- Accidents - dropping the phone, viruses and water damage can cause the settings to be changed.

All of these factors can change a person too, over their lifespan.

Sometimes - in serious cases - the factory default setting has to be used.

This setting will reset everything back to the original store bought mode.

It wipes out all the changes that have been made to the phone.

Changes made by the phone itself, outside influences or its controller/maker.

This book is about how my default settings got changed throughout the 50 years of my life and how the reset option had to be pressed to restore myself back to it's default settings.

You see, if you are too damaged like a phone, resetting is sometimes the only option.

I never wanted this book to be only about myself.

Instead I wanted it to be a learning tool as to what can cause someone like me to be that damaged.

Everyone's life experiences are different.

Life experiences which mould them into who they become and who they are today.

If this book happens to help **one** person then I feel like it has achieved its goal.

In prison I have learnt a lot of things.

I have also done a lot of things here that I would never have done outside.

The most important thing I have done so far is that of studying the Bible.

I quote from Proverbs chapter 9, verse 9: **"Anything you say to a wise man will make him wiser. Whatever you tell a righteous man will add to his knowledge."**

I don't profess to be wise but what I can profess to, is that the lessons learnt and life experiences I have had, **can** and **will** make you wiser and will add to your knowledge!

Besides these blessings you're coming with. I'm really glad to hear from you Mr J. Hope you'll sleep well tonight knowing that your light still shines far beyond the horizon of those cold walls.

Quote from Rasta a released detainee.

The pot of oil

For a long time in prison I was convinced gambling disorder - as defined in the DSM-5 (a manual used by mental health care professionals in the United States) - was the cause of me committing my crime for which I was sent to prison.

In fact, on 16 January 2024, I was officially diagnosed by a clinical phychologist as having the mental illness known as gambling disorder.

But one day after thinking long and hard about it, the realization came to me that the cause of the crime was gambling disorder, but the cause of the gambling disorder was **stress.**

Stress can cause mental health problems.

If you experience lots of **stress** this may lead you to develop a mental health problem such as anxiety or depression.

Stress can be relieved in many ways.

Recreational drugs or alcohol are unhealthy examples of ways to relieve your **stress.**

Good examples are exercise, vacations (only certain types), animals, socializing, sex, music, sport, reading and writing.

Since I have been in prison, of those good examples, reading and writing have been the only **stress** relieving things I could do.

Apart from the mental health problems, **stress** can cause other major health issues - such as high blood pressure, high cholesterol, eating disorders (either not eating, or eating too much of the wrong kind of food) and sleep apnea and other sleep disorders.

Stress can also lead to relationship problems with friends and family.

They say that having a drug addiction will eventually lead you to prison or the grave, but in my opinion **stress** can do the same.

Look at the number of people that have committed crimes due to **stress**, or have died from a heart attack or a stroke from too much **stress**.

I have likened **stress** to oil in a pot.

The pot containing the oil is being heated on a gas burning oven top.

Everyone's default setting is to have some oil in the pot.

That small amount of oil helps you to complete tasks and makes you feel more energized.

Through various events and traumas the oil in the pot increases in volume.

To decrease the amount of oil in the pot, you need to de-stress i.e. do things to help lower the oil level in the pot.

A problem arises when the oil fills to the top of the pot and starts bubbling over, causing a fire - which leads to either permanent damage or the whole house burning down.

So when this happens we get damaged, go to prison, or we die!!!

Let me take you through my pot of oil......

Birth

I was born in 1971 the last of five children - a mistake, I was told.

The first addition of oil to my pot happened only hours after my birth.

I was vomiting blood.

The hospital staff had forgotten to give me the vitamin K injection.

All new born babies are given a vitamin K injection to prevent a serious disease called hemorrhagic disease of the newborn (HDN).

Without the injection it can lead to dangerous bleeding which in turn can cause brain damage or even death.

In my infancy I also suffered from ill health in the form of asthma.

I went to lots of doctors and spent a lot of my days sick in bed.

It also affected my sport life but it became a lot better when asthma pumps came into operation.

Asthma causes obvious stress from not being able to breath.

So oil level ◇.

I was born and raised on a five acre plot in Putfontein, just outside Johannesburg in South Africa.

It is the same place Charlize Theron was born and raised but unfortunately I never knew her!

The plot was a kid's haven with plenty of places to explore, lots of animals and plenty of exciting activities to do.

We had a swimming pool, a tree house and a zip-line plus home built sports fields to play cricket, tennis, golf and soccer on, as well as unusual sports like croquet and tennikoits.

We also had plenty of animals as my mom bred fox terriers and siamese cats.

There were also dangers lurking such as snakes, big hail stones and fires.

The plot had over a hundred almond trees and every so often a fire would break out and everyone in the area would assist to put it out.

It was safe and secure in those days but one time escaped criminals ran down our driveway chased by the police!

That was scary!

The one year it actually snowed, which is unheard of in this part of the world.

I remember sitting in class and the teacher shouting," Kids it's snowing! Run outside and play!"

You didn't have to ask us twice to go and play in something we had never experienced before.

When I got home, my brothers were allowed outside to build a snowman but for some reason I wasn't allowed to go outside - maybe it was my illnesses?

———————————

Walking into the prison cell I was afraid of what I was about to encounter.

It was 22 March 2023.

The court had set my bail hearing for two days later.

So in the meantime they sent me to St. Albans Correctional facility in Port Elizabeth, until the outcome of the hearing.

I walked through the open prison door of the cell and a hundred and twenty faces stared back at me.

Five of the faces were white like me but the rest were various shades of brown to black.

Race has never been a personal issue for me - we are all human beings no matter what our race, creed, sex or religion is, **but** *this is South Africa, a country with a racist history like no other country on earth.*

White supremacists established laws in this country so that people of color were segregated to live apart from the whites. Innocent people were sent to jail, who dared to fight against the oppression.

A white man in this country is hated by the other races for the things his white forefathers did.

Even though my Dad fought against apartheid it will have little consequence, as all that the other inmates will see is a rich racist white male!!!

I took in my surroundings:- the cell was about 140 square metres in area, with an additional bathroom section comprising of two basins, three showers, one urinal and one toilet.

The cell was built to accommodate a maximum of 40 people so clearly 120 was a bit much!

As you are reading this, you are probably thinking "Who cares? These are ruthless, murdering, thieving, raping, child molesting, low lying scum of the earth! They don't deserve any better."

But *these were trial detainees.*

*All those people in that cell were **innocent** and yet to have a fair trial.*

Imagine if it was your son or daughter who was falsely accused of some crime, or setup by other evil parties.

(There will be true stories of those kind of cases later in this book).

I stood there in the doorway of the cell and opened by big mouth and shouted, "THERE IS NO WAYS I AM SLEEPING HERE. I AM GOING TO SPEAK TO THE HEAD OF PRISON!"

I was quickly told to shut up!!

I was in the quarantine cell.

A cell where all the newcomers and first timers came to for a few days before they got assigned to a permanent cell.

I soon discovered that not all of the detainees were newcomers, but some were battled hardened gang leaders who were there to recruit and get what they could grab.

So the guy who told me to "shut up" started strip searching me and my possessions, but I had nothing of value (value being either cigarettes, money, drugs, food, expensive designer shoes, anything that could be traded for their drug of choice).

After they had finished rummaging through my stuff, I sat down in the only open space I could find.

But they were not finished with me yet!

I was called to the back of the cell to a place which is called "the stairs".

This is where the big guys of the 28 gang did their business.

The opposite side was "the springs", the home of the 26 gang big boys.

I was nervous as all hell.

I mean I had never even been near a prison in 50 years and now I had to face this nightmare!

The gang leaders wanted money from me so I could secure a bed.

A bed was obviously very important as about 60 people would be sleeping on the cold concrete floor that night and for some nights to come.

I must explain that the section of prison we were in was the old maximum section of the prison, which was probably over 50 years old without any maintenance work ever been done to it.

The maximum sentenced prisoners complained to the courts about their living facilities, and in 2015 they were moved to the newly built trial section.

The trial detainees who clearly had less human rights, were moved to the old section.

The walls, floor and roof were all solid concrete, cold in summer and freezing cold in winter.

The dirt was packed on the floor from years of various kinds of dirt being trodden in, without cleaning, never mind the various insects!!!

So paying for a bed was a no-brainer.

The big guy gave me a phone to get hold of my wife with.

He wanted R200 airtime.

But my wife was not responding to spam calls as she had been inundated with them since my arrest.

I sent her a text and they gave me a bed so long to share with another white guy, while we waited for her reply.

Later on, around 11pm, things in the cell started to change.

Sleeping arrangements were now about to be sorted out.

The white guy with me was moved to the floor and he was replaced with a big black guy who took over his space and most of mine as well.

Eventually I was half-off half-on the bed which was the top bunk, and falling off would not be fun!

How was I going to sleep?

BTW the next morning the big black guy told me that he was there for a rape charge!!!

I shouldn't have worried about sleep as nobody in the cell was allowed to sleep.

The gang leaders made sure of that!

They walked up and down the pitch (the name given for the aisle) making a noise and messing around with the people - the drugs they were on, probably crystal meth or cat, did not let them sleep.

These were guys half my age!!!

I managed 30 minutes of sleep before six o'clock which was when had to get up.

The rest of the day was a complete blank for me, as together with no sleep I didn't get my medication.

But later on that day I ended up in my permanent cell with only 70 people in it, but this time they wanted R1000 for a bed!

Welcome to prison Jonathan Simon Blow!!!

Early childhood

In 1976, at the age of 5, I was enrolled into grade one at junior school.

No pre-school or nursery school for me like my siblings had experienced.

My mom or dad obviously thought that as my sister had taught me to read and write, that I didn't need pre-school.

Even though emotionally I was never ever ready.

Throwing me in the deep end can only cause the oil level to rise.

So oil level ◈.

At this age, Easters and Christmases were exciting and wonderful celebrations in our household.

My mom went all out to make sure it was a special and memorable occasion.

At Easter time she would hide Easter Eggs all over our big garden.

Chocolates and sweets were scarce in our house so finding them was even more exciting.

The one time she enlisted my Grandma to help her hide the eggs.

Grandma was already quite elderly so when we couldn't find all the eggs we asked her where she had hidden them, but she had forgotten!!

My mom followed the German tradition of Christmas, which meant a stocking night on the night before Christmas Eve.

The stockings were stocked to the brim with small toys and sweets and we would wake up at the crack of dawn to open them.

She would make a massive feast for supper, like seven different foods, and afterwards we would go outside to look for Father Christmas.

When we had supposedly seen him and the reindeer, we came back inside to find all our presents stacked next to the Christmas Tree.

God bless my mom for all the effort she put in to make these occasions special.

My Grandma was also a very special person in my life and I would spend hours with her in her caravan, which she stayed in for a while on our plot.

My parents would go overseas for work and she would take care of us.

We spent hours doing puzzles, crosswords and listening to the radio.

She also helped me to enter a competition on the radio.

One day I was phoned by the radio station, as my name got drawn out for the competition of the day.

I remember the DJ asking me if I lived in a box as the address I had written on the entry letter, was a post office box address.

Anyway he asked me a question which an adult should know, so I ran inside and asked my mom for the answer and guess what? She got it wrong!

Nevertheless they sent me a hamper of chocolates in the post, which for a young boy, was heaven!!!!

———————-

When you are in prison you are assumed to be a criminal whether you are guilty of a crime or not.

You are a criminal by process of association and your situation.

I never ever felt like a criminal - the talking by others of their crimes they had committed made me angry and sick.

Your mindset does not have to be the same as those around you - whatever your situation is.

Stick to your own morals and principles even if you are there for a crime you did, as it may have just been one mistake or one bad influence.

Prison dishes up its own special kind of bad influences.

The first crime I was asked to assist with was from the big black possible rapist, who shared my bed on the first night.

He asked me how to go about stealing money off his company expense card he was given (Like I was an expert in fraud all of a sudden).

Now in any situation you are faced with I believe you have three choices:

1. ***Take the high road***

Try a positive approach to lift up the other person to make him or her a better human being. In other words convince them that crime is not good.

2. ***Remain neutral***

Don't give an opinion either way. This is probably the best way to react in a dangerous situation.

"I don't know", is the best reply.

3. ***Side with the devil***

Take the easy road, thereby bringing the person down and lowering their morality and human principles of decency and kindness. In other words help him commit the crime.

I remained neutral.

This was not the time to take risks - if I took the high road he may have become angry with me and done me some harm, and - if I sided with the devil then I would have been angry with myself for aiding and abetting a crime.

So my simple answer was, "I don't know".

The next time I was asked to commit a crime was when I moved into my permanent cell in the section.

My paid bed was next to one of the big guys in the 28 gang, Allen.

I will write in more detail about Allen later in book.

He asked me if I knew of any houses in the rich areas which could be robbed, and whose owners were away regularly.

He actually grilled me!

I pretended not to hear what he was asking but he was persistent with his questions.

At that time I had a sinus infection and my left ear was deaf, so I didn't even have to pretend not to hear.

My go to answer was, "you are mad to try and steal from the rich houses as the armed security is extremely vigilant in those areas".

I remained neutral.

You have to do that when you are surrounded by gang members and have no where to run to!

He told me that so many of the crimes outside were committed by trial detainees.

When I moved to single cells I thought I would get away from questions about helping commit crime, but that wasn't the case.

A fraudster in single cells grabbed me during exercise times and grilled me about security systems and controls in retail businesses.

I was tired of even giving him the time of the day!

My standard answer was, "you can't steal from those businesses, their systems are too good!"

Going to court was the same.

Guys would try and talk to me about the best ways of committing further crimes.

Here is a suggestion for the authorities - why not put an undercover person in prison to find out what crimes are being planned and stop them before they happen?

Clearly throwing criminals together leads to more dangerous and daring crimes.

There is the thrill of the crime that makes these criminals addicted and they get off on hearing about other people's crimes.

It's like if you have a business meeting about marketing your product, everyone in the meeting throws their ideas on the table and through mutual consensus you get the best idea.

Imagine if those were criminals around the table?

The crimes they would come up with would be of a high standard!

Proper criminals should be isolated - it's clear and obvious.

Also, why are prison cells not separated according to certain criteria such as:

- *type of crime;*
- *number of crimes committed;*
- *age of the offender;*

- *religion;*
- *mental state;*
- *illnesses*
- *education level*

The list goes on and on.

Good influences can only help bad people.

No question was asked when I arrived in prison, either in trial or in maximum, as to where the best place for me to stay was.

I know its difficult to know where to put people but the state has phycologists and social workers to assist in fitting people into their "box".

The results will be mind blowing!

———————-

Jonathan

There were a lot of Jonathan's in prison.

This Jonathan helped me a lot.

He did everything for me and in reply I helped him out with his case and urgent stuff he needed.

As far as I could tell from the information I got from him and his co-accused, Jan, he was innocent.

I got a lot of information about their case as they wanted me to practice with them as to the details of the events that led them to prison.

I still don't know what the 100% facts of the case are.

They stayed in a farming area in a huge farming community in South Africa where apples, pears, apricots, peaches and other fruit, grew in abundance.

The area was and is ravaged by crime, mainly theft and murder fueled by crystal meth's users.

Jan was looking after a farm on behalf of the State but the farm house was a target for the "tik" users.

So Jan decided to take the law into his own hands as the police were not responding to the crime.

Jonathan worked for Jan on the odd occasion so he was used to taking orders from him.

One weekend he took Jonathan with him to the house to keep watch and catch the criminals.

Jan had a gun so he was well prepared.

Two guys broke into the house in the early hours of the morning while Jonathan was keeping watch.

He woke Jan up who grabbed his gun and apprehended the first guy, tying him up with cable ties.

As Jonathan was tying him up, the 2nd guy appeared with a big knife about to stab Jan.

But Jonathan shouted to Jan in warning.

Jan turned and shot the guy before he could attack him.

The guy died almost immediately.

At that stage sanity should have prevailed but people make mistakes and panic.

They put the living guy in the car and the body in the boot, in order to take them to the police.

Something made Jan, who was the driver, change his mind about going to the police.

Instead he drove to the forest and dumped the body there.

He then decided to leave the living thief in the forests 100km's from town, making him walk back as punishment.

The next night they went back to move the body, strip him of his clothes and throw them and the weapons away.

The car was also washed....

The kidnapped thief eventually made it back to town and went straight to the police station!

Of course the two were arrested.

Something in the story doesn't add up, but from my point of view Jonathan was an innocent party.

In fact he was a hero - he saved Jan's life!

They are accused of murder - Jonathan never shot the gun, attempted murder - Jonathan never owned the gun or car, kidnapping - Jonathan never owned the car and took instructions from Jan

Pointing a gun - Jonathan never owned a gun

After a couple of months in prison, Jan was let out on bail but Jonathan wasn't!

This shocked me to the core.

In fact Jonathan spent another 5 months in prison before he got bail.

I am convinced Jonathan is innocent and should be given credit for his actions.

He should have been on the news for his heroics instead of sitting in prison.

Their case is still ongoing and I am interested to hear the outcome.

Jonathan is a good man and he has had a hard life, but I know the Lord will bless him.

Violence

The years between 1978 and 1982 were filled with violence and trauma in my house.

My dad had major issues.

I think a lot of it was due to the mounting **stress** caused by his job, his big family he had to support and his extra-marital affair.

We never knew what to expect from him.

He was unpredictable and a total autocrat.

He ruled the house according to his rules.

Everything he said was obeyed or was supposed to be obeyed.

In those years there were four teenagers in the house - a normal father would battle to keep peace and order, but my dad wasn't normal.

He reacted to problems in a violent way.

His punishment would be severe - a hiding with a belt and then banished to your room forever.

Sometimes you were never even aware of what you had done wrong.

I don't think my siblings or I were bad kids.

We were just normal, going through changes that all kids go through.

The one time he had my mom cook rabbit for supper, but she was not allowed to tell us what we were eating.

Meals were very formal occasions.

We were made to sit properly, use the right utensils and obey all the manners that were customary.

So we all ate the meal and actually it was delicious.

When my dad asked how it tasted, we all complimented the meal.

Then my dad let the rabbit out of the hat, so to say, and told us what we had eaten.

My sisters were horrified, burst into tears and stormed out the room.

We grew up next to a rabbit farm and there was a bunny park in our town, so eating one was never going to go down well!

His escape from **stress** was horse racing.

During those years he taught me about horse racing and gambling.

To escape **stress** and violence in the house, I would take form guides and study them - play betting on past races.

I would also listen to music, like the Beatles, which was hugely relaxing.

Even at a young age I had to find ways to de-stress.

Another one of my favorite activities was playing ball games on my own.

Spending hours hitting a ball against a wall, left hand versus right hand.

One day I was hitting the ball against the wall of the lounge area (I don't know why I was so close to the house, normally I would go far away), when all of a sudden my dad charged outside, smacked me hard across the head, and shouted, "I TOLD YOU TO STOP THAT!"

But I had not heard him say anything.

I cried so hard that day, but I swore that after that day I wouldn't cry again.

I wouldn't give him the satisfaction!

Sports and games - in my experience, were great things to take your mind off real life, as your focus was only on the task at hand.

When my father broke my brother's nose in front of me it triggered a hugely stressful event in my life.

I was only 11 years old and being exposed to that kind of violence at home, leaves a scar.

I can remember the incident clearly, even some 40 years later.

He also came home one day and started smashing out all the windows of our French doors.

I think my mom had locked him out of the house due to his affair.

My brother eventually stopped him by hitting him with some object.

During those years my other brother also went through some major trauma.

A friend of his had come to visit and at the end of the day, they went to wait for his parents on the main road at the end of our long driveway.

Apparently they were running across the busy road when a car hit my brother's friend and killed him.

My brother witnessed the whole incident.

The driver of the car was unlicensed so he was charged with capable homicide.

I would definitely say my oil level was higher then it should have been after the first ten years of my life - even though I had used gambling, music, sports and games to try and reduce the **stress** levels.

The aggravating factors of the first ten years were more then the mitigating factors, so the oil level had to go ◈.

————————-

For someone opposed to violence in all its evil forms, prison is not the best place to be.

The people I was with had different backgrounds to me.

Backgrounds where violence was part of their lives, inbred into their very souls.

That's how they learnt to deal with challenges & frustrations.

A fight was a big thing in the cell, like a school playground where kids crowd around a fight trying to grab a glimpse of the action.

Also the noise of a fight stands out from other noises in the cell and prison.

A concrete floor makes the sound of stamping feet echo throughout the cell - the walls would reverberate the sound of fist against flesh.

I never personally witnessed any really violent fights but there were a few in the cell during my time there.

Fighting was a huge no-no in the cells, for obvious reasons, but what astounded me the most was how the violence was dealt with.

*The offenders were called to a disciplinary meeting by the glas (glass) and the draad (wire) - every gang section has a **glas** (who is the person who sees everything that goes on in a cell), and a **draad** (who is the person who disciplines the wrong doers in the cell).*

The glas would detail the crime to the judges (senior members of the gang) who would hear from witnesses and then pass sentence on the guilty parties.

The punishment for less serious crimes would be a slap in the face with a hand or a slipslop.

They would get numerous slaps, first one cheek and then, ironically, the other cheek.

The more serious crimes got dealt with by a beating with a bag full of soap bars.

I never witnessed this, thank the Lord, but I heard the screams of anguish and the crying afterwards.

What didn't make sense was they were trying to fix violence with violence!!!!!

I even suggested other forms of punishment, such as cleaning duties or a threat to move them to a die-die cell (where the mad people were placed).

But violence was a traditional way of punishment and like our government they will never change to more effective and intelligent forms of punishment.

Weapons for fights were not available **except** for hot water from a kettle.

There was a fight in my cell where one convict decided to throw hot water on the guy who was irritating him.

For some reason these guys were not disciplined, maybe because they were injured and had to get bandaged at the hospital.

But the prison officials banned kettles after that - the majority suffer for the foolish behavior of a few!!!

Allen

Allen was one of the first guys I met in prison.

Allen had a big smile on his face when he met me.

He was so friendly and he wanted me to come to stay in his cell.

I met him when I was still in the "quarantine" cell, so I decided to go to his cell as I didn't know any better.

First impressions tell you a lot about a person and normally I was pretty good at sussing out someone new.

But I wasn't experienced with criminals and Allen was a hardened criminal.

He also discriminated against people and I could see he had a thing against the whites.

His crimes were stealing and house robbery from white, rich people and his attitude was that they could afford to get robbed.

With some people the more you get to know them, the more you like and respect them - they grow on you.

The opposite is also true.

My first impression of Allen was that he was a nice friendly guy, but my opinion of him changed over time.

When I was brought into the cell he made sure I was given the bed next to him, supposedly for protection.

He didn't explain any rules to me and I think it was on purpose.

It gave him leeway and power to shout at me when I did something "wrong".

He did that lots of times.

The first time I was half asleep and walking back to my bed from the bathroom.

I bumped into two guys talking furiously to each other.

Allen grabbed me and pushed me hurriedly into my bed area, saying, "I told you not to go near those guys grrrr".

Huh????

First of all he never told me anything and secondly what did I do wrong? (Months later I found out they were busy with "Siko", a "prayer" time in the morning but it was more an information sharing time between the two gangs)

The next time he admonished me was when he saw that the curtain on the window between our two beds was open.

He said, "You are supposed to close the curtain!!! You are an old man!"

Huh?

Once again I knew nothing about it (he wanted the curtain closed to prevent the wardens from seeing him talking on his phone)

The third time, I was called into the "stairs" by him and told to sit.

He went off at me about how I was supposed to be an example for the young guys and that this was his fucken house (excuse the French).

I didn't have a clue of what he was talking about.

But I had brought a packet of cigarettes from the 26 gang and apparently that was not allowed.

I had to buy from Allen but they never had cigarettes to sell, so he's argument held no water.

I was seriously shouted at but I was never told the rule in the first place.

Before my first family visit Allen sat with me and made up the food list for my family to bring.

He went with me to the visit to help me collect the stuff.

I thought he was helping me but of course he wanted the food for himself.

I had about 2 items out of four packets full of stuff **brought** by **my** family - it was the first and last time I asked for packets of food.

*After every family visit I had, he took boxes of smokes for **himself** and not for the guys in the cell.*

Allen had three wives and kids in different parts of the province and they kept him busy, especially between the hours of 10 and 12 at night.

I would go to sleep at 9 o'clock at night and Allen would be fast asleep already.

At about 11 o'clock when I was sleeping like a baby, he would shake me awake and tell me to light a smoke.

*We would smoke and he would talk for hours about **his** problems.*

This became a form of bullying for him as he did it regularly, enjoying waking me up and smoking my cigarettes.

I began to despise him.

It's funny, as soon as your opinion changes about someone - you despise everything he says or does - you have lost respect and it can't be won back.

I just wanted him to leave.

The last week before he left he helped himself to my food and smokes again, making hay while the sun shone.

He was 100% sure he was going home.

Unfortunately he got 6 years imprisonment.

I haven't spoken to him since.

Bee attack

The bee attack!

1982 was the year of the bee attack (I can see my wife rolling her eyes as she reads this).

It's a coincidence that a swarm of bees attacked me as I had "researched" the topic a year prior to the attack.

I was like Nostradamus - BTW, I also thought I would end up in prison somehow!

Nostradamus reminds me of a teacher I had in grade 4, Miss Muller.

I will never forget her, as on her first day of teaching ever, I vomited all over my desk which was situated at the front of the classroom.

You see I still had an illness I had contracted while on holiday, Encephalitis.

Encephalitis is the inflammation of the brain.

It's the worst illness I have ever had with massive headaches and vomiting.

So I caused panic for Miss Muller on her first day.

I digress, the reason I mentioned her was because she would tell us stories about her brother, whom, she said, could predict the future and see things such as ghosts.

She once told us that her family were driving somewhere when they stopped at a traffic light.

Her brother made a prediction that there was going to be an accident happening at that intersection on that day.

True as Bob when they returned, there was a serious accident on the scene.

I don't think - in hindsight - that the stories she told us 8 and 9 year olds, were appropriate.

Nevertheless, one day I got hold of my dad's encyclopedias.

In those days there was no Google so all your research was done out of the encyclopedias, A to Z, or at a library.

I researched "what to do if you are attacked by a swarm of bees".

The instructions were clear.

Firstly, if a swarm of bees approaches you angrily, don't run - lie down flat on the ground and don't move!!!

Secondly, if that doesn't work (and you are stung to smithereens), then get up and go and jump in the closest body of water.

Things often work out the way God plans and not in the way you want it to!

On the bee swarm attack day, it was my friend, Gavin's birthday party.

His mom was at school to pick us up, me, Gavin and Robert, his other friend.

We made a bad decision to rather walk to his house - which wasn't far from the school - instead of accepting the lift.

We crossed over the first road and walked straight into a swarm of bees (apparently some boys had been throwing stones at the beehive in the tree)

I instructed Gavin to lie down as Robert sprinted away.

The bees proceeded to sting us everywhere using us as a pin cushion!

The first option definitely wasn't working.

I told Gavin to get up so we could try to find a pool of water, urgently!

The first house we tried we were chased away angrily.

But the next house we found a pool and our friend Robert!

We jumped in the pool and got rid of the last of the bees.

Needless to say I was very sick as I reacted very badly to the hundreds of stings, and what's worse I didn't get to go to the party!

The "bee attack" increased my oil levels and anxiety levels, and I now had to watch out I wasn't stung by a bee ever again!

———————-

An amazing thing about this South African prison system is that no reading or education material is given to the inmates.

Reading is an important part of development, progress and increasing your knowledge.

There were plenty of people I met who either wanted to learn how to read, or read interesting material - material which could possibly remove them from a life of crime.

A large number of guys couldn't read, so isn't this the perfect time to teach them?

I mean six year olds can read - it's the first thing a school kid gets taught.

It's a huge failure by our Government that adult people cannot read and it's no wonder that they are in prison - what work could they possibly get without basic life skills?

I brought reading material from memoirs to fiction novels, life inspiring books and books where people's dreams came true.

And the books were popular - not only did it educate and inspire them, but it helped to pass the time.

Books have always been an important part of my life.

From a very young age I was reading novels such as the Faraway Tree, Secret Seven, Famous Five and Arabian Nights.

My great, great, great, grandfather, John, was an English composer and appointed organist of Westminster Abbey in 1668.

In 1685 he was named private musician to King James II.

My grandfather, Ernest, published the first science fiction novel in South Africa in 1963.

My dad, John, worked with books most of his life.

His job was manager of paperbacks for CNA in South Africa, so he travelled a lot - sourcing books locally and internationally for sale.

This job meant he received a lot of books for free and he always brought them home for us to read.

I remember going to his office in Johannesburg and would spend hours looking through all of the new books he was given.

So books was and obviously still is, a huge part of my life - why should prison change that?

I always wanted to write books and especially a book that could potentially change someone's life.

You may think that you or your family will never end up in prison but it's not impossible - if you are at the wrong place, at the wrong time, you could end up here pretty easily.

What happened to me, could happen to anyone.

Learn from this book please!

The one thing about books is that you have to look after them, as they can be read again and again, and handed down to future generations.

My inmates did not look after the books - in fact they destroyed them and smoked them.

But at least the books helped a few of them!

When it comes to things to do in a prison cell nothing at all is provided by the State.

Do they expect inmates to smoke drugs all day, or fight, or plan their next crime?

No TV, radio or even a kettle was provided in a cell - prisoners can, under strict conditions, bring in their own.

This is okay for sentenced prisoners but how can an inmate on trial bring stuff in, if he could be sentenced or sent home at any time.

It's ludicrous!

The other thing that blows my mind (excuse the pun), is that no sheet or blanket is given to you in the trial section.

At least you get two sheets when you get sentenced, but still no blanket!

So what do they expect inmates to do? Steal?

A very basic need is warmth so how do you get that without a sheet or a blanket?

Blows

My

Mind

Farming

1983 - was another stressful year for me.

My dad had had enough of his problems in the business world and wanted to buy a business, far from the hustle and bustle of Johannesburg.

So I was moved out of grade 7 (my final year of junior school), after the 1st term.

We went to our new business which was a farm in the Tsitsikamma.

Talk about being thrown in the deep end once again!

I was enrolled in the local Afrikaans school where I was taught one on one by the principal, the only one in the school that could talk English.

Apart from attending the new school, I had to work on the farm in my spare time.

My dad made me help him with selling fruit and veg, this was called "smousing".

Going to farms and the market at four o'clock in the morning to buy produce to resell.

This was a time of no money - the farm battled to make ends meet and there were no luxuries!!!

So the oil in the pot ◈.

That first year on the farm was also fraught with me waking up at night to loud noises.

It was the sound of my dad hitting and shouting at my mom.

I was only 12 but I reckon the pot was already half full with oil.

Everyone asks me about the notorious gangs, namely 26 and 28, or pumalanga and shonalanga.

These are the gangs that rule the prison.

Gang members are by far the majority in prison.

My understanding of gangs is that they are there to protect you, make sure everyone has something and are taken care of.

They work on the principles of discipline and respect.

People have the wrong impression about the gangs in prison and of course there is always the exception to the rule.

But the truth of the matter is that prison wouldn't work without the gangs.

Unfortunately the gang leaders in the trial section abuse their power and use the gang members to fill their own pockets and drug consumption.

They also prey on non-gang members - stealing their valuables, especially phones - as they know that there is nothing that can be done about it.

Money and "stock" collected by the gang leaders are supposed to be accountable and shared in the form of a ration to the lower members.

There are ranks, just like an army, in the gangs - I don't know how you move up in the ranks.

I have heard rumors about stabbing wardens and having sex with the top ranking guys, but I have never experienced this first hand.

Rules of the gangs are not explained properly to any new guys and that results in problems.

But you feel safer under the protection of the gangs as long as you tow the line.

Gang protection was very important for me and was necessary at maximum.

One thing they instill repeatedly is discipline.

In a way, gangsterism is just like brainwashing, and if brainwashing is for a good thing, it is ok, but it can turn out badly if it's not for a good cause.

Brainwashing about discipline is a good thing in prison as it promotes:

- *Cleanliness*
- *Hygiene*
- *Neatness*
- *No fighting*
- *No shouting at each other*
- *No encroaching on each others*
- *Being ready for court and meals on time.*

The young guys in the trial section did all the cleaning and washing of clothes.

In maximum everyone takes turns to clean, including the big dogs.

I paid someone to clean for me!

<u>*Types of Criminals*</u>

For ease I am going to split criminals into four categories, namely:

Bottom feeders

Money makers

Stagnators

Rise Abover's

All the criminals I have met fall into one of these categories.

Let's look at each of these categories in more detail:

Bottom feeders

These criminals are at the **bottom** of the food chain.

They came with **nothing** and still have nothing.

These guys are the real **criminals** and there is not much that can change that.

Their **mindset** is of a criminal nature and how to get their grubby little paws on other people's stuff.

They are the real criminals inside and **outside** the prison.

They have no **family** support and they pretend to be **friends** with others, just to get something from the relationship.

They are happy to live off prison **food** and have to scarrel (beg) to get a **luxury** (a smoke, tobacco, food, drugs etc.)

They are - false; liars; devious; bad to the bone.

Their motto is, "to ask costs nothing".

These are the people that tormented me.

Money makers

These are the people who are there to make money.

They have people working for them and are most definitely at the top of the **food** chain.

They were successful outside, making money out of illegal activities, so they are not going to let prison stop them in their quest to become **rich**.

These guys are the most dangerous **criminals** of the lot as they will stop at nothing to get what they want.

Their **mindset** is that of a criminal, what can they sell you at a criminal price, never minding the condition of what they sell.

They have lots of **support** outside to assist them in getting their products to sell.

Their **friends** are all people that could help them to make money.

They live off the **luxuries** they get from various contacts.

These guys do not usually smoke or take drugs.

They are fake, scrupulous, aggressive and selfish.

Their motto is, "I will get you anything with the right money".

Unfortunately I needed these people to get smokes, food and other necessities.

<u>Stagnators</u>

These criminals are somewhere **between** the bottom and the top of the food chain.

They have **no direction** in prison which reflects how they were outside.

They don't really do anything but they don't **scarrel** or beg from you.

They just go about their business, sometimes getting a visit, only to have some of their stuff taken from them.

They do smoke and take drugs.

It's part of their no ambition in life, hoping drugs would help them get through the bad times.

They are lazy, unambitious, quiet and sad.

Their motto is, "hopefully somebody will rescue me".

These guys don't give you problems and on the rare occasion, you can promote them to the rise Abover's category.

<u>Rise Abover's</u>

These are not **criminals**.

They shouldn't be in prison.

They are either **innocent** or they made **one** mistake.

They were successful outside or were on the way to success.

They have loved ones from all spheres who support and visit them.

They are organized and have all they need in prison.

Unfortunately, they are prime targets for the guys in the money makers and bottom feeders categories.

They do everything responsibly and they don't do drugs.

Their motto is, "don't give up and do something in prison to make you better".

I was one of those.

———————

Addiction in prison is rife.

Drugs users are plentiful and you can see they are addicted as they show all the signs.

They wake up and the first thing they do is take their drug and at night they need to take their drug to help them sleep.

Much like gambling was for me.

And when they don't have their drugs they go through withdrawals and become angry and aggressive.

Drugs are freely available but sometimes the money to buy the drugs, is not.

They have to get the money from someone and they try non-stop to get from you.

A packet of cigarettes will get them the hit they need as they can trade them.

The more hard-core the drug is, the worse the withdrawal symptoms are.

It's not only drugs that they are addicted to, it's also crime.

Crime gives you a similar high to a strong drug.

They told me how they get the thrill of walking around another person's house in the dark and it's even better if the people are at home.

That's why they cannot stop.

When you are an addict the fear of imprisonment is overridden by your addiction - just like with me.

Your rewards centre of the brain takes over and the decision making and cognitive thinking part of your brain plays second fiddle.

Once again, the State needs to address the source of crime and by doing that these addicts won't come back to prison again.

Becoming an addict doesn't happen overnight - in fact it can take 50 years of various trauma events to transform a normal person into an addict.

All of us have the predisposition to become an addict, so look for the signs in yourself and others.

———————————-

<u>Ranking of things asked for in prison</u>

You get consistently asked for stuff in prison.

It's annoying but you can understand as some people don't have the means to get anything of their own.

I have ranked the top five things, in my opinion, that are asked for the most:

In fifth position is <u>sugar</u>.

A highly sought after commodity inside and outside prison.

Prisoners want sugar for their coffee, tea, hot water, porridge and cereals.

And when they asked for a spoon of sugar they usually took three!!!

In fourth position is <u>toilet paper</u> or waste as it is called.

Another sought after commodity inside and outside prison.

Yes we do get provided with toilet paper but one roll every two weeks is not enough.

But some prisoners waste the toilet paper on using it as a light for their drugs or they use it to dry their eating utensils.

In third position is a pen.

Yes a pen!

I went through about a hundred pens during my stay at the trial section.

A pen would get lent and never seen again.

I soon learnt to lock up my pens!

In second position is cigarettes.

A valuable trading commodity.

You can use them to buy sugar, food and drugs.

I wish I never smoked as my life would have been easier in prison.

But you were hounded day and night for a cigarette or a piece of one or a puff of one or the butt!

In first position is .... a lighter!

The majority of prisoners smoke something in prison and they can afford to buy their drug of choice.

But they can't afford a lighter!

It was easier for them to ask me.

Even in maximum it was the case and I spent hours lighting other people's stuff.

———————-

Vudu

This guy was a leader of the 28 gang and he took his job seriously.

He was ruthless with the young guys instilling discipline and respect into them.

He told me he was in prison from the age of thirteen and had been in and out since, over 22 years

You could see he was a hard-core convict.

But he was also a drug addict.

I estimated he smoked up to 3 tablets of mandrax a day

He would smoke it in the cell at night, next to me and my lungs would breath in this thick, disgusting smoke.

Sometimes he would vomit from over use.

He had nothing in life so the only way he could get money for drugs was by scarelling off lower gang members.

He asked me a number of times for money or smokes for his tablets.

Without them he was an angry man and anything could happen in the cell.

You could see he was getting sick and the last thing I heard about him was that he had contracted TB and was in single cells.

Wiseman

This is a big big black man who stayed next to me in single cells.

What a good guy!

He was anti-gangs, anti-smoking, anti-drugs and alcohol but he loved food!

I shared a lot with him but he always paid me back.

He taught me a lot about how the gangs worked and also about politics.

He made me understand the black culture.

He definitely didn't belong in prison.

He was in single cells as he fought with the gang members but he stood on his morals and principles and with the right opportunities can go far in life!

Hostel

1984 - I was sent to hostel in Uitenhage, a small town outside Port Elizabeth.

For a lot of boys going to hostel was fun as they were getting away from their parents (a lot like how prisoners here feel).

The first three years of my hostel life was hell for me - I just hadn't found my groove.

I wasn't good at anything.

I was battling with academics, sport and socializing.

In hindsight I think the preceding years had taken its toll on me, and I had become an introverted nerd!!!

The first day I walked into hostel I was given the name "Blow job".

For a long time I was super proud of the name until I found out what it meant, and then became super angry at the sound of it, lol.

In those days the grade twelves or matrics were known as fagmasters, and they would choose a grade 8 to fag for them.

Fagging involved making their bed, folding, hanging and packing their clothes, carrying stuff for them and even sitting on the toilet for them to warm the toilet seat.

I didn't last long with the first matric as he tested me out with hanging some clothes, which I had no training in.

I failed and was happy as I had no fagmaster!

But Rico, who I refer to below, found out and got me to fag for his fagmaster so he could do nothing!

I was also averse to violence and in those days the masters and the seniors would dish out hidings, with a cane or a plank.

I had suffered with bullying from my older brothers when I was young.

The older boys in hostel also loved to bully, especially bullying the nerds!

There was a guy called Rico who was in grade 8 with me - I was 12 and I think he was 15.

He would walk around naked in the dorm.

Sometimes he would grab me and dry hump me on the bed!

He did lots of sick things like that.

Those three years my stress levels increased and I also had no release from the stress - every 3rd weekend and holidays I went back to the farm to work.

The next two and a half years were much better and I started to thrive.

I always felt like I was at least three years behind everyone else.

The only major stress factor for me was when I smashed my elbow in rugby in my final year of school.

At the end of grade 11 the school chose the leaders of the school, the prefects.

It was customary for the parents of the newly chosen prefects to be there, to witness the announcement.

I knew I had a chance of being a prefect but when I looked around my parents were no where to be seen.

So I had that sinking feeling that I was not going to be a prefect and I knew my friends were going to be prefects, so I was unhappy.

But to my amazement my name was called out, a total shock!

The question is why my parents couldn't be there, as everyone else's were.

My good friend, J, was the main reason why I started to thrive.

My sporting, academics and even girls took off like a rocket!

J and I played lots of sports in those years, golf, tennis, soccer, baseball, badminton, table tennis, the list goes on.

In my first year of university I started to gamble again but it was just a form of entertainment.

That feeling as a student that you can do what you want.

My Friday mornings would consist of golf, tennis and then a trip to the local horse races.

The races were mainly to rekindle that happy feeling I had as a child, watching my dad work on his passion and the joy he got from it.

My friend Garth, started a "company" with me where we combined our bets and expertise to give us a better chance of winning - that didn't last long!

So those two and a half years the oil levels came down.

The first half of my first year at university, I was thriving, but that didn't last long.....

————————-

Put yourself in a position of a waiting trial detainee for a moment .....

You have absolutely no ways of communicating with the outside world.

You were ripped from your family life without warning, leaving them to fend on their own.

The state kept you in prison, denying your bail, but by being in prison you have no ways to fight to get out of prison - one of many ironies in life.

You are not allowed a cell phone in prison.

There is only one logical reason for that - you can threaten or kill witnesses or other people involved in the case.

But if you wanted to do that, then you could get your people to come visit you and give instructions face to face.

The people who do those kinds of things are the minority.

The majority just want to keep in touch with family, friends and their lawyer.

Regardless of the fact that no cell phones are allowed, people like Allen will always get one and use it to commit a crime.

Surely a better idea is for the authorities to allow phones and monitor any suspicious behaviour?

Then they can deal with those perpetrators with punishment, such as solitary confinement.

Deal with the wrong doers and not the innocent.

I mean if the public phone systems worked, which it hasn't for two years since 2022, there would be a way for everyone to contact their loved ones and their lawyer.

So the only "legal" contact is through a once a week visit or when you eventually get to go to court.

The wardens say you can use the office phones, but every time you ask them they give some poor excuse.

I have never been able to use a prison phone for those reasons.

Most prisoners don't get a visit and their court dates can be as much as six months apart.

So they cannot communicate with anyone for a long long time - and they don't even have necessary toiletries.

You get desperate to speak to a lawyer and when you see him or her, it's a five minute hurried discussion.

Lawyers do not visit you in prison.

Because you cannot communicate effectively, the State always has a 90% advantage against you, even though you are entitled to a fair trial.

Another problem with communication in prison, is that the prison officials don't tell you the rules and the laws pertaining to that section of the prison.

On trial and in maximum I never received any rules.

Another irony of prison life is that you have to find out the rules from fellow inmates - talk about the blind leading the blind.

They can tell you anything and you will have to believe it, as you don't know any better!

There is a thing called "counting" in prison.

This happens every morning and every night, in trial.

In my opinion, it's the most pointless exercise in the world.

And the amount of times they count us incorrectly is scary!

Three of them count us and still they get it wrong.

Each time they count, the 70 people in the cell have to stop what they are doing or wake up from their sleep to get counted.

In maximum you still get counted but it happens when walking back from mealtimes - an easy seamless process.

I'm not sure why we get counted because there is nowhere we can go!

Another important communication tool in prison is the P21 request.

This is a piece of paper, as scarce as hens teeth, where you write your requests to the head of prison.

But there are never P21's available and you are not allowed to write on blank paper.

I did a number of requests when I was on trial, namely:

● Move to single cells 1st time - this was approved the same day;

● Move to single cells 2nd request - there was no formal denial of this request but verbally I could tell that the people in charge were not keen;

● Move to single cells 3rd request - this was approved after I got tired of waiting for the 2nd request to be approved!

● A request to see an outside dentist - this was declined ;

● A request for a kettle - approved.

I also made some requests in maximum, namely:

● A request for single cells - verbally declined;

● A request for a non-smart tv - approved;

● A request for toiletries - approved;

● A request to teach - this was declined. No reason given.....

Death

July 1989 - my father passed away.

This sent the level of oil in the pot up a few notches.

My dad was an extremely heavy smoker throughout his life, smoking cigarettes and tobacco.

He also never exercised and loved food!

In my matric year I noticed he was battling with his breathing.

I would sometimes make him laugh, then he would pass out from lack of oxygen.

His face would go blue and his tongue would stick out.

All of a sudden he would come out of unconsciousness and wonder what had happened.

He went to hospitals for tests but he checked himself out.

He obviously knew he was sick.

My parents were always discussing selling the farm and moving inland to the karoo, where the air was better for a person with lung problems.

They were too late.

The most problematic factor of his passing was that he left nothing behind for his family.

My mom, who had never worked in a full time job before, was left stranded on a farm that was worth almost nothing.

So the next years up to 1995 were stressful.

I now had the added burden of my mom's well being, as well as having to work to pay for my studies and to live.

To cut a long story short, I managed to get my chartered accountant qualification in the prescribed seven years - but with a lot of stress and not many de-stressing activities.

———————

You think a lot about death when you are in prison. Your situation demands it.

Surrounded by violent murderers and gangsters, no love and support - only suffering.

Death is on your doorstep.

Infectious diseases and no medication. Sometimes you wish you were dead.

Death ....

Three people that stayed with me in my cell were killed outside after they were released from detention.

Vuntu - who I will talk about in more detail later on. He stole a cellphone as he was hungry. He got a six months sentence and was released after two months. A month later he was shot and killed after gunmen came to his house to kill his brother. They shot him instead.

RIP my man.

Mapinz - a big guy who was full of life. I met him in my early days of prison. He was a taxi driver. His case was thrown out of court. The day he left prison, I asked him if he was going home. He said maybe but he didn't want to go home. Two weeks later he was shot dead.

RIP big guy!

Burelo - A man who was always organized, a rise abover, who had lots of support outside. He was on trial for five years. He was released after he was found not guilty. He was going to be a rich man as he could claim from the State for the five years he was detained. Instead, after a few months of freedom, he was gunned down.

RIP Bhuti!

Crime and violence are both realities in prison and death becomes a reality.

Some guys have been detained in the waiting trial section forever - it's like they have died and been forgotten about. The one guy in my cell had been there for seven years already. And my other friend, Myna, who I will write about later, has already been in this hell for five years.

You are entitled to a speedy trial in this country, as per the Law, and those people are innocent and have been denied bail.

The other issue is that for some reason in South Africa, time spent in prison waiting trial means nothing. It is not seen as a punishment and therefore, not taken off your sentence.

So these guys will spend between five and ten years in a place where your human rights are violated and then they get sentenced. They will have to do their full sentence on top of the trial sentence.

It's madness I tell you.

Something is wrong with our Law - either give the person bail or take the time off his sentence that he spent waiting trial.

After your first year in prison nobody contacts you or visits you.

You are alone, in the hands of an incapable State lawyer.
<u>*Timmy*</u>

Timmy was the first guy I met in prison who actually showed real concern for me. In other words he wasn't after something for himself - a rare specimen.

I'm not sure for what he was on trial for, all I know was that he had been there for four years and when he was arrested he was a full blown drug addict. Crystal meths, mandrax, coke etc.

He told me that he had made a conscious decision to give up drugs and spent the first three months in solitary confinement to help him break the habit.

After that he came to a cell where drugs and smoking was rife, but he survived it. He stared addiction in the face and beat it.

He told me to take one day at a time and in the evening he would say," You see the day is over!"

He always knew he was going home.

He had belief.

Anything I asked of him, he would help with pleasure.

His good mate was Mpinz who went out of prison the same time, so they enjoyed some parties until Mpinz was killed.

Thank you Timmy for your humanity.

A functional family

June 1995, I got married to my beautiful wife, Jo.

I had been dating her since 1989.

We had met at a varsity party.

She noticed me across the crowded room and wouldn't leave me alone after that!

Lol, I'm joking, it was love at first sight.

She has stuck with me through ups and lots of downs but she still believes in me.

Love conquers all!

Her family had taught me what a functional family was supposed to be, and it helped me a lot being around them.

They did a lot of things together as a family and to my surprise there was not much fighting and violence. We could even finish a board game without too much drama.

My mother-in-law gambled and often she would take us with her to the closest casino, which was two hours drive away.

It was my first encounter with slot machines, machines that would later ruin my life!

1997 - was the time for my first overseas trip and my first real holiday in years. (I have added in my overseas trips as it's important to always plan a holiday that will decrease your stress and not vice versa)

Jo's family had planned an American trip which included a visit to Disneyworld, New Orleans, Chicago and New York.

In my opinion it is very difficult for someone with high stress levels and high anxiety, to fly.

It was my first long distance flight and my anxiety levels were pushed to the limit.

On the flight to America - about 24 hours in length after a stop in Amsterdam - I did not sleep.

It put me in a dazed state for the first few days.

Although amazingly enough we got to see a space shuttle take off the day after landing.

The problem with flying somewhere is that it is difficult to enjoy your holiday.

At the back of your mind you know you have a long flight back to endure.

On that trip my father in law and I, actually missed our flight from Orlando to New Orleans - that added to the stress!

I got to visit my brother in Chicago and he shed some light on my upbringing - my father's abuse and his affair. A lot of the details I was completely unaware of.

Although it was very nice to see the States, the vacation did not decrease my stress at all!!!!!!

———————-

I loved food until I got to prison.

Cooking was a relaxing pastime for me and at one stage, during covid, I was creating my own recipes.

I like bold flavors, spicy and tangy - my favorite ingredients are chilli, garlic and lemon.

The last time I saw those ingredients was March 2023.

In prison the food is bland and cold and no love is put into making the food. At home you can taste the love.

At home you can eat as often as you want, like five or six times a day. Snacking on healthy food. In prison you get two meals a day, one at 8 and another at 3.

You do not look forward to the meals in prison but a lot of prisoners do!

Some even try their luck and go back for seconds!

Niekie (who I will talk about later) loved the food and sometimes he would have three helpings. He pestered the cooks for more food and sometimes he got a plate or some bread thrown at him.

Talking about bread, it became literally the only food item I ate in prison and it was always brown and never fresh.

Breakfast you got one slice of bread and for lupper you got a quarter loaf bread. When I got sentenced that changed to eight slices for breakfast and none for lupper.

The rest of the food was boring - porridge for breakfast and samp or mielie meal for lupper.

Sometimes you were lucky and got an Apple or pear for breakfast or even a boiled egg!

Vegetables was the worst part of lupper.

It was either boiled cabbage or boiled carrots, although on the odd occasion we did get beetroot or butternut.

The protein was either burnt bony fish, a chicken, beef or pork piece or a polony sausage - the size of the helping was minute, it could have filled a fly!

The plastic dish they serve the food in doesn't help your appetite - in fact it does the complete opposite.

To drink in the morning you get disgusting tea or coffee and hot watery powdered milk.

For lupper you get some funny tasting cooldrink.

The majority of the time I gave my food away except for the bread and the small piece of protein.

Giving the food away caused problems of its own as everyone wanted my food!

I was told by the big boys that I could only give my food to certain people. So I made a list of those I could give to and made turns to give to them fairly.

We eat with our senses. Think about it for a moment......

• Our eyes see what we are going to eat and if it looks delicious we will eat it with pleasure. Prison food, however, looks disgusting.

• Our nose smells the amazing aromas making our stomachs grumble with anticipation but prison food smells like shit.

• Our ears hear food being cooked, the sizzle, bubbling, frying and other noises associated with cooking. It anticipates ourselves for what is about to come. In prison you never see and hear the food being cooked.

• Our touch can indicate how the food is cooked. Is it crisp and firm and ready to eat or soft and squishy like prison pork?

• Finally our taste can override all the other senses, because if it tastes good we will enjoy it, despite everything else. Thus the taste of the prison food confirms what the other senses have discovered.

Outside I lived to eat but here I eat to live!

<u>*Myna*</u>

Myna had been on trial for five years when I met him.

A young guy who had learnt all the bad habits of prison.

He had nothing.

He was involved in a double murder case with four other guys, three of which were in prison with him.

At first he didn't annoy me or ask for stuff, that started when he moved up the ranks in the 28's.

He was one of the guys who took stuff in excess.

Like sugar - if he asked for sugar you were assured he would take four heaped spoons!

But he didn't smoke so I did share some food with him.

He took advantage and sometimes he would ask for my locker key to get some butter, but when he was in there he would grab a snack and quickly eat it.

I wanted to get him back for this and by accident it happened.

Chilli sauce was a prized possession and one day I managed to buy some.

It was a bottle so I reckoned it could last a month.

It arrived and the guy that got it from the shop took a third for himself.

Myna's eyes lit up when he saw it and my heart sank - deep down I had hoped that he didn't like hot stuff.

The very first meal after I got the sauce, he asked for some.

But he hadn't even tried it yet.

So I poured a lot on his food as he liked a lot of someone else's stuff.

I watched him as he ate and then his nose and eyes started to run!

His chewing became slower as his mouth was numb and on fire!

He looked at me through the tears and we both burst out laughing.

Gotya!

Our relationship became strained as time went on.

He did nothing to help me, instead he sucked me try and also he was very loud and ignorant of people around him.

I lost my temper with him a few times and eventually he was moved out the cell.

It was a lot better when he left.

I have heard from him since and he is still waiting for his next date for court!

—————————-

LOVE

'Love is all around us, it's everywhere we go"

Lyrics from the song by the band Wet, Wet, Wet and it also happens to be my wedding song.

But where was the love in my home where I grew up?

Maybe my dad the autocrat had issued a command," Thou shall not talk about love or say I love you in my house!'

I wouldn't say it was a loveless house but, except for Christmas and Easter, there was no sign of it.

My dad had a British background and ancestry.

He grew up never talking about his feelings and this transferred to his offspring and home.

Telling your children that you love them is of vital importance.

It's affirmation otherwise how else do you know?

As of today I still don't know if my parents loved me, my mom possibly and my dad, possibly not.

The fact is that by not being told leaves unanswered questions in your mind and now it's too late to ask them.

As a result my siblings and I grew up with an inability to express our feelings.

The stats show that we have five out of five divorces (even though mine was for legal reasons)

The divorces could have something to do with our inability to express love?

Our **default setting** is that we are made and born with only love in our hearts.

A baby does not know the meaning of hate or indifference.

So when do these anti-love feelings occur and from where do they come from?

In my case these feelings were injected by my brothers from an early age.

Bullying can cause that to happen.

Being smacked around was supposed to toughen me up and cowboys don't cry?

You could have beaten me everyday and it still wouldn't have made me into a tough guy.

Your family, friends, social media, TV, radio etc, all have influences over your anti-love feelings.

If there is plenty of love in your home, those bad influences won't affect you much - like a wall of protection around you.

In fact you can then influence others positively with love.

"Your life must be controlled by love, just as Christ loves us". Ephesians 5:2

One of the most popular quotes from the Bible is, **"Love your neighbour as you love yourself"**, Matthew 22:39.

The important part of that quote, for me, is "as you love yourself".

One of the six types of love as defined by the Greeks, is self-love.

You need to love yourself first.

You need to look in the mirror everyday and say, "I love myself and am happy with who I am."

I didn't love myself for 50 years and for I long time I hated who I was.

My life was ruled by an addiction and I hated it.

Prison changed that.

If I had a mirror, I could look in it now and say I am happy with who I am now.

My mind is clear.

I learn everyday and help people all the time.

My body, mind and spirit is a hundred times better then what it was under the power of addiction.

I have two friends who exemplify love and they leave you in no doubt as to their feelings:

<u>Big Boy J</u>

A man I have known for 25 years who has only got better (and bigger) with age.

He told me and our friends that it is ok to say "I love you", to another male friend.

The machoness of males prevents this from happening, but why?

If you love someone why not tell them?

Don't be worried about what other people say, this is your life.

Big boy J is a friend in a million and has an awesome attitude towards life and love.

He is super popular and he never has a bad thing to say about anybody.

I miss the music trivias we did together where he would always make me sing and chase the crowds away!

He has visited me in prison, one of the few, and has supported me throughout.

Isn't that what love is about?

Thanks for you love big boy!

<u>Zee</u>

Zee is another person who wears her heart on her sleeve.

She is so popular because of who she is.

A funny story - our daughters played waterpolo together so we often travelled together. One day we were driving with her, when her phone rang. (that was always a dangerous thing as she lost focus on the road)

She answered," Hello my darling? How are you my sweetie pie?.

And then after the person replied she said," OH you are just the best, I love you!"

I thought she was speaking to one of her kids or a new man in her life.

It turns out she was talking to her builder!

Someone she had just met.

But that's Zee, a human being bursting with love!

So you see there are people like them in the world.

Friends like Stiffler, Crazy fowl and Lompies have been great support but others have disappeared.

In prison love is hard to find.

If anyone shows you love, then they normally want something.

Maximum is a bit different and there some people actually do show love.

"Love is patient and kind, it is not jealous or conceited or proud. Love is not ill mannered or selfish or irritable. Love does not keep a record of wrongs. Love is not happy with evil, but is happy with the truth. Love <u>never gives up</u> and it's faith, hope and patience never fail.

Love is eternal."

Corinthians 13:4

Our pigeon pair

September 1999 - my first child, Julian Alexander, was born.

What an experience it was to see a live human appear out of Jo!

I was there to witness the miracle of his birth.

When I took one look at him my immediate thought was this boy is alert!

And that's what he turned out to be and he always asked 100 questions - at meals we actually started counting his questions and there were a lot.

He did not give us any trouble as a boy and has been a pleasure to have as a son.

He was diagnosed with mild to severe depression and I never really understood his mental illness until I was diagnosed with my own.

I now understand what he goes through on a daily basis and it's not easy.

He has made me proud!

Your **stress** levels go up with children - all the added responsibility and worry!

Oil in the pot ◇

June 2000 - I was employed into an extremely **stressful** job, as a credit manager for a multi-million rand company.

A credit manager has to be one of the most **stressful** jobs around. The **stress** comes from the reliance you place on the 150 plus clients to pay you, not just once a month, but up to 4 times a week.

As a result your job is not judged monthly like everyone else. It is judged weekly.

Every week my job was judged by the top brass, all the way up to head office.

Mondays became a nightmare for me, as that was the day I checked bank statements to see who had not paid.

The amount of unpaids could run into tens of millions and **stress** is caused by factors beyond your control.

When the Financial director position became vacant I applied, as that was my natural progression.

I saw the credit manager position as a stepping stone to a position which suited my qualification.

I didn't get the job and the main reason given to me by the managing director was that if I wanted the job, then I should have been acting like the financial director already.

It was a confusing answer as I had my own job to do, which took up all my time, so how could I manage that?

Besides the old financial director would never had let me interfere.

Oil levels steadily increased ◇

Oct 2002 - my second child, Emily Cate, was born.

Pile on the **stress**, and Emily was one of those toddlers that increased your **stress** levels.

Once again I bore witness to her birth, and once again it was a miraculous experience.

One look at Em and my first thoughts was that she was feisty!

And that's what she became.

As much as Julian was a quiet boy, Emily made sure she was heard.

As a toddler she was active and was walking at 9 months.

She gave us lots of scares climbing up anything she saw.

She became that energetic, feisty player in the pool and excelled at water polo.

I was in prison for her 21st, a day a father looks forward to.

She had made me proud!

We have always been a close family and believe that if we stick together, we will not be defeated.

Joanne has had a lot to do with the way the kids have turned out and that stems from her family upbringing.

Love you guys!

2003 - I was diagnosed with high blood pressure and high cholesterol.

Along with those issues, my weight was too high - those symptoms are all a result of high stress levels.

—————————-

For an old man like me, 52, exercise is important.

Especially with health conditions like high blood pressure and high cholesterol.

Doctors, health workers, dieticians all tell you to exercise on a regular basis, like 30 minutes minimum per day.

Exercise has always been part of my life and my daily routine - I mean golf is exercise, right?

Why should prison be different from the outside world? - all the amenities that are here have open ground, gym equipment, soccer balls and lots of time!

I got so used to exercising outside, like speed walking for an hour in hilly areas.

I expected that to continue in a bigger way in prison - and why not?

Why wouldn't a prison promote exercise?

Even though there were about 1500 detainees, there were enough wardens and time to ensure we got an hour exercise in the sun, daily.

But this was too much to ask.

Instead we got an hour every ten days!

The other problem with prison exercise is that other prisoners don't see the allocated time as exercise time. They see it as a time to "scarrel" for stuff (smokes and drugs) or to kick the ball around aimlessly.

Even in maximum (where you get an hour a day), I would try to at least walk around the block, but would be stopped by other prisoners - even those in my own cell. They have 24 hours a day to talk to me in my own cell, as we are locked up together but they choose exercise time to harass me!

The first time I went to exercise I made the mistake of taking cigarettes with me and soon as I lighted one up, the gangs crowded around me - note to self don't take cigarettes to exercise!

So I got no exercise on those days.

In single cells you got exercise more frequently but only the one shift of wardens, for some inexplicable reason, gave us exercise.

So you would get on a Mon & Tues, nothing on Wed & Thurs, and then again on Friday and the weekend. Vice versa the following week.

The same thing would happen there - I would be walking briskly and then someone would stop me and talk to me for the next hour.

The best exercise I got was in my single cell where I setup my own exercise program.

It helped a lot but I miss my walking with my wife and her friend - listening to their stories of the day and trying to get a word in edgeways!

Prison is punishment but why does exercise have to suffer?

<u>*Trust*</u>

Trust is definitely in our default setting.

We Trust our parents or our guardians to keep us alive - to feed, clothe, bathe and care for us.

Trust is completely putting yourself in somebody's hands and expecting them to do the right thing.

I went to a training course once, where the course leader made us do a simple exercise:

- close your eyes

- fall backwards

- the person behind you will catch you

It's a scary feeling waiting for that person to catch you.

That's trust in a nutshell.

When you are blind they help you to see.

The trust we are born with, can either get stronger or it can break altogether - the funny thing with trust is that it takes only <u>one</u> untrustworthy action to ruin <u>thousands</u> of trustworthy actions.

"I trust nobody" is what a lot of people say.

What a load of rubbish!

It's impossible to go through life without trusting anybody.

Every time you get into a car, a plane, train or ship, you are trusting the people who made it and the person driving it.

<u>*But*</u> *if you trust someone and that person fails you, then who is to blame for that?*

You can be in a position of trust for 20 years, do thousands of trustworthy transactions, then get sick with a mental illness causing you to break that trust.

That's what happened to me.

I was asked, "how could I break the trust of the victims?"

What was the cause of me breaking the trust I had built up over 20 years, was it:

(a) I felt like throwing my life away?

(b) Greed and jealousy?

(c) A mental illness diagnosed by professionals

There is only one logical answer for that (c)

Trust works both ways.

In business there is always a mutual trust, you provide goods or services and in return you get payment.

I trusted the victims that they had made sure their systems were working properly and that their employees did their jobs correctly.

That was their responsibility - something a real man would have admitted in court.

I took responsibility for my actions but they didn't.

Was I the only one at fault?

Neither of us benefitted from the crime.

But a system is there to pick up irregularities in case something goes wrong with the system or people.

Here is an example of what can go wrong in a business. A plan suggested by a fellow prisoner:

He suggested kidnapping an accountant or accountants who would then provide him with unlimited access to their bosses bank accounts.

So through no fault of the accountant, the money of the bosses will get stolen.

Is the accountant/s to blame?

No and the bosses systems should pick up the theft quick enough to limit the theft amounts.

The point here is that things happen to people which are out of their control.

What happened to me was out of my control and there are many cases like mine. People who were: lawyers, bookkeepers, CA's, investment bankers, church accountants, politicians, people with high standing in the community.

Risking your business on one person is totally unfair on that person.

He can only lose.

When things go right, he was supposed to do it, so he is not rewarded.

But when things go wrong, he will be punished forever.

That is why people in Canada, UK, USA and Australia don't get harsh, unrealistic sentences for this specific crime.

South Africa should follow suit of these countries and institute repayment orders - the victims then benefit from the sentence.

Courts in those countries recognize that this illness can do serious harms to individuals - causing good, honest citizens to commit a crime.

In prison trust issues abound.

I was told not to trust anyone in prison.

But you have to, it's impossible to go through the hell of prison without help.

I have a test which I do which can be used in the outside world.

If someone wishes to borrow a box of smokes with a promise to repay them, then trust them to do so.

If they don't repay you when they said they would, then don't trust them again.

You know where you stand with them.

It's a costly lesson but one you have to learn.

Trust someone until that trust is broken.

I trust that God has laid out my path for me and no matter what I try and do, I can't change that.

"Then Jesus said to the disciples,' and so I tell you not to worry about the food you need to stay alive or about the clothes you need for your body. Life is much more important than food, and the body much more important than clothes. Look at the crows, they don't sow seeds or gather a harvest, they don't have store-rooms or barns. God feeds them! You are worth so much more than birds. Can any of you live a bit longer by worrying about it? If you can't manage even such a small thing, why worry about the other things? Look at how the wild flowers grow, they don't work or make clothes for themselves. But I tell you that not even King Solomon with all his wealth was clothed as beautiful as one of these flowers. It is God who clothes the wild grass - grass that is here today and gone tomorrow. Won't he do the same to clothe you? How little faith you have. So don't be always upset, concerned with what you will drink and eat. Your Father knows you need those things. Instead be concerned with his Kingdom and he will provide you with those things.

Trust in God.

Luke 12:22

Flying

Sept 2004 - I had had enough of the corporate life so I decided to venture into another highly **stressful** job - my own accounting consultancy business.

If anything was going to be more **stressful** than a credit manager, this was the job.

This **stress** is different - it comes from having to put food on the table.

Also you have to work long hours to make it successful.

The other huge negative is that your relaxing holidays are mostly gone!

At this stage of my life the only gambling I was doing, was in the form of poker clubs.

These were fun, once a week occasions and not a lot of money was gambled.

I was too busy with work and a new family to get distracted by the noise in my head.

2005 - came my next holiday vacation.

Even though I couldn't really take a holiday, it was my 10 year anniversary. A very important milestone in our marriage.

If I had high anxiety from flying before, then this trip sealed it!

I was also at the highest **stress** point in my life thus far so I needed a romantic holiday.

The flight was doomed from the beginning - all the signs were there - from missing passports, a hair raising trip on the back of a bakkie in Johannesburg an airport under massive maintenance.

Due to the maintenance, we stood in the queue for ages - then to top it off, Jo and I were split up.

I sat in the "bubble" on top and Jo sat at the bottom with complete strangers.

We were 30000 feet in the air, about 30 minutes from Johannesburg, when I heard a loud bang coming from the airplane door next to where I was sitting.

Apparently the noise was so loud downstairs that the air hostess in business class dived onto the floor!

You always watch the air hostesses in a situation like that - the one at top with us, who was busy serving drinks at the time, took one look at the door and ran out the cabin.

Meanwhile................. I grabbed the drinks trolley.

The noise coming from the door was so loud on top that we couldn't even hear the announcements.

Jo told me later that the captain had announced that one of the door seals (the door next to me), had faulted.

Here is the news report of the incident:

SAA aborts flight for technical reasons

Johannesburg, South Africa, 9/25 - A South African airways (SAA) flight bound for Mauritius Saturday morning, was called off due to a technical reason, the airline confirmed.

"At no stage were any of the 331 passengers on board the Boeing 747-400, in any danger", said Jan Blake, SAA technical and operations head.

SAA 190 departed Johannesburg for Mauritius at 9h39 local time and had to make an in flight turn back 20 minutes later after shear rivets on a small panel inside door two on the upper deck failed and the panel opened.

"To the best of our knowledge this is the first time an incident of this nature occurred on the worldwide Boeing 747-400 fleet", Blake said.

SAA said it would report this incident to the Civil Aviation Authority (CAA) and Boeing as this may result in a one-time inspection of the Boeing 747-400 fleet.

The passengers will stay overnight in Johannesburg to depart again tomorrow morning, the airline said.

(Source - www.pprune.org)

————————-

One of the things I struggled with in prison was my medication and especially getting treatment as and when you needed it. I mean if you are sick now, what it the point of going to a doctor 5 days later? Medication is there to either cure you or relieve your symptoms that you currently have. The symptoms may be gone in a few days.

I'm in pain today so I need pain relief today and not next week!

When I was arrested I was on four different types of chronic medication for: Asthma, high blood pressure, high cholesterol and anti-anxiety and depression treatment. Never mind the other tablets I used to take such as pain, stomach and allergy meds - those are medications you normally keep at home for ease of use. My medication created an immediate problem for the court. I made sure they knew about my chronic meds as I knew they would become a problem in prison, whereas it wouldn't be if I got bail. When I was sent to prison the first time my chronic meds went missing and for three days I never got them. They had been sent with me but not in my possession. The police needed to handle them and give them to the hospital section, who in turn would give them to me. They were chronic meds, meaning they needed to be taken by me to prevent a asthma, heart, blood or psychotic episode. So for two days I got nothing.

I asked the wardens but they didn't care.

After my bail hearing, which was postponed, I requested not to go back to prison as they couldn't give me my meds. I was kept in a police cell for about three weeks where I had no problem in getting my meds. After that my bail was denied, so off I went back to prison to spend time with the "general population".

Once again my chronic meds were with me and for the first couple of months things went smoothly. During this time I developed chronic sinusitis from all the five different kinds of smoke in the cell. I was quite sick as the infection had spread to my ears, throat and lungs. To go and see the doctor was a mission and what makes it worse is that you just want to sleep, so going to the doctor is not your priority. Eventually after a week of suffering I got to see the doctor, if that's what he was. He never even examined me. All he did was ask some questions about my chronic meds and prescribed me some weak pain and allergy tablets. I didn't get the meds immediately instead I had to wait another three days to get called to collect them. But it wasn't worth the wait, the tablets did nothing for me. I battled until the medication was finished and then I started trading cigarettes for any stronger pain blocks I could find - I had no other choice. One day I was in such pain and I had no tablets. But an angel arrived with tablets and I survived to live another day in prison!

My sinus infection was not going away so my wife got my doctor outside to send some proper sinus medication. That took another week to get!

My next batch of chronic meds were not allowed into prison. The hospital said the wrong name was on the boxes of meds. But they were looking at the pharmacists name which was on the top of the label and my name was clearly highlighted on the bottom. So I never had chronic meds for three weeks. Eventually I was called to court and my lawyer got a court order demanding that the prison let my meds in.

It got better from then onwards but every now and again I would not get my anti-anxiety tablet.

The worst pain I went through was severe leg pain which lots of prisoners got. It comes from not exercising your legs anymore so your muscles cry out in pain. The worst thing about this pain is that it would come in the middle of the night. I remember being woken in single cells to the sound of someone crying in the cell above me. He was complaining about how sore his legs were. I also had the same pain so I knew how it felt. When I was moved back to the section a guy called Laz came to me begging for pain blocks. He said his legs were in pain. I said, "My man I know what you are going through!"

I gave him some tablets but every night he came back for more. His name was written down to go for treatment for two weeks but he was never taken. That's how it worked, sometimes you got lucky and sometimes not.

The pain tablets they gave you were no stronger than panado. My pain continued when my tooth broke in early December on a hard pork bone.

It wasn't sore but more irritating.

I immediately wrote a request to see my dentist outside as there isn't one to be found in prison. He apparently makes his appearance during a blue moon. My request was denied and I was told to go to the hospital - for what? A pliers to pull my tooth out with?

I left it as it was not painful, yet......

The pain started when I was eating pork again. And this time the pain was immense.

What could I do?

I couldn't go to the dentist and I couldn't pull my own tooth out.

And it was not only my tooth that was sore. It was my ear, neck and throat.

Jo managed to organize me antibiotics from my doctor outside together with some strong pain meds.

Unfortunately the antibiotics did not agree with me and I vomited non stop! I had to stop taking them and relied on the pain meds rather.

I was waiting for my sentence and then hopefully I could get to see the dentist.

When I was sentenced and went to maximum section, the nurse at the hospital laughed at me when I asked to see a dentist - "a dentist", he said, "you will wait a long time".

The pain got worse in maximum and I never had pain tablets.

I got given new asthma pumps and new blood pressure tablets. They didn't have my anti-anxiety meds so I had to stop taking them.

It's a great place not to have those kinds of medication - maximum security prison!

An unexpected overseas trip

2007 - was my next overseas holiday. A holiday which came out of the blue when my stress levels were high. One of the victims of my crime won a trip for two on a Mediterranean cruise. His wife was pregnant at the time, so in desperation he asked me to go.

Contrary to both victims court testimony where it was stated I was given holidays(plural), this was the only one and it was for free for the victim. It's not that I didn't appreciate the offer, but I am sure one if his brothers should have rather gone.

Flying after 2005's incident was murderous and on top of it the flights were extremely bumpy.

Once again a holiday is supposed to be stress free but not this one.

Luck would have it that the Monaco grand prix was happening on the day we docked into Ville Franche.

Of course we had to check it out as the grand prix was fifteen minutes train drive away.

We couldn't get tickets for the grand prix as they were sold out, so we sat in a pub close to the action.

Things went pear shaped very quickly.

The tequilas started flowing.

We had to be back on the ship before seven pm, so in our drunken state we left at five for the train station, in plenty of time.

Luck, would have it though, that there was a train strike that day and the queue was around the block.

Our next option was a taxi but there were none to be found in Monaco.

The last option was the bus.

The bus stops were like a feeding frenzy.

A bus would stop and fifty people would try and cram on at the same time.

We must have waited an hour to get on the bus and on top of that, we missed our stop!

When we finally arrived at the harbor the ship was sailing away in the distance and there was no way it was ever going to turn back for us.

We were screwed!

The trains did not go to our next port of call, Livorno, so we had to take a taxi - an extremely expensive trip.

But we never had a choice.

We stayed in a seedy hotel that night and the next day, thank goodness, we made it back onto the cruise ship.

Talk about stress!

2009 - I was not in the best physical shape.

Apart from my asthma, high BP and cholesterol, I was overweight, tipping the scales at over 100kg's.

Every diet I tried, even the disgusting cabbage soup diet, didn't work.

I was also having sleeping problems, snoring very loudly, and waking up in shock, struggling to breath.

I needed to sort it out as I was constantly tired and irritable.

I went to the sleep clinic to get tested and I was diagnosed with sleep apnea.

Now sleep apnea is extremely dangerous for your health as your body produces adrenaline hormones to shock you out of sleep so you can breathe.

The hormones increase BP, cholesterol and of course, <u>stress.</u>

So I had to buy a CPAP machine.

A machine that gets plugged in, attached to your mouth via a pipe and a mouth piece and produces oxygen which gets pumped into your body.

It opens your airwaves allowing you to breathe easier.

I did not take to the machine!

I struggled to fall asleep with the noise and the contraption that was stuck to my mouth!

I persevered and some nights I got some good sleep.

My main focus was to lose weight because that could fix the sleep apnea!

The oil in the pot was increasing still.

———————————-

Vuntu

I met Vuntu when I arrived in my communal cell.

He had his own way of doing things and didn't care about what other people said about him.

I liked him and we soon built up a friendship.

He wasn't a dangerous guy, he just committed his crime as he was hungry and also had the added responsibility of looking after his special needs brother.

I think he had lots of potential.

The one thing he was good at was collecting things.

He would have a big bag of rubbish collected throughout his year's stay.

The other thing he collected was jewellery.

He wore a lot of jewellery inherited from his mom.

The perfect job for him was in the jewellery industry - I promised to buy him a metal detector for his birthday.

Sadly he died before then.

————————

When days are dark, friends are few.....

A friend in need, is a friend indeed......

Unconditional love.....

The question I ask is," If your family member or friend ends up in prison, what is your reaction?

I don't think this is a grey area, it's black or white.

*You either support them and find out first hand from them their story and help where ever you can, **or** you believe everything you hear and read and discard them like a piece of rubbish.*

That person has no more use for you.

Discarding them is acceptable to society.

This is how you are supposed to treat an offender.

Lock them up, throw away the key and let them be rehabilitated by the system.

After their punishment is done then maybe you will accept them back into your life.

Sticking with them is the hard road, like the road to heaven.

Society will not approve and will say things like, "How can you associate with a person like that?

Look what he did. He deserves to rot in hell."

It's interesting.

In my case, the press were there for every court appearance, whether trivial or important, __except__ when I spoke.

When I told some of the true story they were not interested.

I even asked the media to write about gambling helplines in their articles, but I was ignored.

I'm not judging anyone, that's definitely not my place __but__ I think the majority of society wants to throw the criminal away, because they themselves are not perfect and have committed some undiscovered crime along the way.

They have done something wrong in their lives and the guilt is eating them up.

That's my only logical explanation because everyone makes mistakes and a good person doesn't all of a sudden become a bad person.

Let's say your family member, for example your brother, who you have known all your life goes to jail.

This is a person you have shared thousands of memories and meaningful conversations.

You are blood!

You have helped each other in life - it hasn't been one-sided.

You loved him and spoke highly of him to everyone.

News breaks about his crime.

Of course you are angry with him.

Angry because he never told you about it, which is understandable.

But there surely must be reason for it.

He always told you everything.

Ask him!

Ask those questions which can help you make your own mind up instead of being a sheep and following society.

I have never discarded anyone without good reason.

Hundreds of people told me their problems and asked me advice and I <u>listened</u> to them.

I gave my best advice.

I am a good person, I know that.

I did one bad thing, does that now make me a bad person?

Some people stuck with me even though they hadn't even heard my story.

That is Faith, which God speaks so much about in the Bible.

It's knowing in your heart that the person is good and nothing can change that.

Others have got the story from me and have made their own mind up, and that's OK, make those decisions but first have the facts.

What I went through is a long complicated story.

But hear the story from the horses mouth.

I forgive my family members and friends that have thrown me away.

If they read this book maybe it will convince you either way of how good or bad I am.

I am here in prison.

I am going nowhere.

———————

<u>Judging</u>

"Only God can judge you"

You see and hear that saying a lot in prison.

It's written on the walls and spoken about.

Unfortunately we are on earth..

There is no doubt that God will one day judge us, but that is only after we have left this life.

On earth, judges and magistrates are in put in positions to make decisions on the future of a person's life.

We all chose this legal system and therefore need to be respected.

Judging one another is a problem.

Matthew 7:1 - 2 says,

"Do not judge others, so that God will not judge you, for God will judge you in the same way you judge others. Why, then, do you look at the speck in your brother's eye, and pay no attention to the log in your own eye? You hypocrite! First take the log out of your own eye, and then you will be able to see clearly to take the speck out of your brother's eye."

Our default setting is not to judge others.

In that passage of scripture the important point is that you have to be able to see <u>clearly</u> without any flaws of your own.

But we all have flaws, nobody is perfect, so therefore nobody can judge.

There are so many bad influences nowadays that creates this arrogance that some people are better than others.

The naked truth is that society likes to judge as it makes people feel better about themselves.

Unfortunately judging people sells newspapers.

Lots of people that didn't know me would have judged me before I was guilty, due to the way the media reported.

I mean they didn't even ask me a question.

My side of the story would never change the readers mind after the fact - once you are judged you are executed!

So the people that judge the most and are the most vocal about it, are the ones with skeletons in their closet.

The one good thing about prison is that nobody judges you here.

You see when there are no bad influences you only worry about yourself, and not about others!

"Welcome the person who is weak in faith, but do not argue with him about his personal opinions. One person's faith allows him to eat anything, but a person weak in faith eats only vegetables. The person who will eat anything is not to despise the one who doesn't. While the one who eats vegetables is not to pass judgement on the one who eats anything, for God has accepted him. Who are you to judge the servant or someone else? It is his own Master who will decide whether he succeeds or fails. And he will succeed because the Lord is able to make him succeed."

Romans 14: 1 - 4

The dreaded CPAP machine

In 2010 when our kids were old enough, 11 and 8, respectively, we made plans with two other couples and their two kids to go on a trip to Europe and specifically Euro Disney.

My wife had just got a new teaching job and as a result we used her pension money to do a once in a lifetime trip.

The B's and the S's and us planned the trip ourselves. Booking the hotels, flights, tours and other transport, online.

It was great fun planning the trip!

But the scary thing for me was that there were seven flights planned for the trip!

A holiday with all the flights, six children under age of twelve and six adults was not going to be a de-stressing vacation.

I also had the bloody cpap machine to worry about, carting it everywhere and making sure it can plug in to all the various plug sockets.

Of course I couldn't use it on the plane so sleep was out of the question.

Once again I battled on the trip.

The cpap and I were not getting along and this led to tension between my wife and I.

In a hotel room as small as the ones we stayed in, my snoring meant there was nowhere for my wife to hide.

At one stage she threatened to sleep in the bath!

I got home from that trip, tired and stressed.

Between the next years 2010 to 2015, I really tried to manage the level of the oil in the pot, which by this stage was about 3/4 full.

The one way I managed this was through healthy eating and most importantly, long distant running.

I took to running and did lots of half-marathons and as a result I lost weight and could sleep without the dreaded cpap machine.

With running you are bound to pick up injuries.

Mine was an hereditary one.

I was born with big calves which are too big for long distant runners. My friend told me I had cattle, not calves!

What happened was that blood would have to work too hard in the calf area and my feet would get neglected.

This would result in numb, floppy feet - they call it compartment syndrome.

It can be fixed with an operation.

The operation involves cutting the sheath around the calf muscle, in the front, back or both.

To cut a long story short (excuse the pun), I had my anterior sheaths cut by a specialist doctor.

It didn't work so I had to hang up my running shoes.

My friend, Stiffler, introduced me to share cfd trading in these years.

Now share investing and share trading are two different things.

Share investing is long term and share trading is short term.

But cfd trading adds a whole new dimension on normal trading, in fact it turns it into gambling.

Cfd trading you only have to put a percentage of money down and the rest gets lent to you.

So instead of buying a 100 shares of a company, you can now buy 500.

You have to leave a certain amount of money in your trading account because if the share drops below what you bought it for, you end up in a loss position and you have to deposit more money.

You would get an email or a phone call in the morning when the markets opened to say your account was on a margin call and either you needed to sell your shares or put more money in.

Of course I got completely obsessed with this and even went on a few courses to learn how to make more money!

But a gambler won't succeed in this kind of money making activity as he is not disciplined enough and takes too many risks.

That happened to me, I made lots of money but then I lost it all and more!

—————————-

0

For clarification, in the waiting trial section of prison you are allowed one visit per week, excluding public holidays and weekends.

Sentenced prisoners get visits on public holidays and weekends.

Shop purchases are allowed during visits on trial and also it's supposed to be every Sunday.

Sentenced prisoners get a limited luxury item shop during a visit and then a normal shop to purchase once a month.

On trial stuff you can get from visits is much more lenient than maximum.

Although for some reason avocados, oranges , bananas and anything you can buy from the prison shop, is not allowed to be brought in.

So if you want fresh milk for your cereal you have to buy it at the prison shop.

The problem is, is that a lot of the time the shop is out of stock of milk so you don't get to eat your cereal.

What is allowed in is very inconsistent.

One week I was allowed packets of soup and the next week not.

The one time papers for my court case were denied entry, the reason being is that I need to get these at court. Huh?

Going to the prison shop was, firstly, unpredictable and secondly, you never knew when the shop would be closed for stock taking or some other reason.

A lot of detainees brought stuff back with them from their different courts.

This varied from court to court, with some courts allowing everything and some nothing.

One of the most stressful things about returning with stuff from the shop, visit or court, was the security of your stuff.

One time a fellow detainee walked into the visit area and proceeded to pick up my packets.

I stopped him and almost got into a fight.

Another time a guy asked me for a cigarette, but then proceeded to help himself to a full box of twenties.

When I walked back from shop or visits, I had to walk fast and keep my head down until I got to the "safety" of my cell.

If anyone stopped me, I tried to get away as quick as possible - the police wardens were nowhere to be seen.

They would not stop asking me for just a sweet!

Putting the stuff in a communal cell came with its own set of problems and someone "trustworthy" had to look after it while I was outside waiting for the cell door to be opened.

In maximum, limited stuff is allowed in for visits.

No food or smoking stuff is allowed to come in.

Anything coming in had to be requested via a P21.

Even in maximum, prisoners still asked me for stuff when I came back from visits.

Visits, court and shop were stressful, scary times.

Even before you go to a visit, inmates harass you to buy them sweets, smokes, cooldrinks and the list goes on and on and on.

It's funny though, when people come ask me for anything and I didn't have it, they get angry with me!

Like I am lying on purpose LOL

<u>Respect</u>

Respect, I personally believe, is one of the cornerstones of healthy human relationships. Without respect we have murder, rape, theft, adultery, molestation and all the other evil things us humans do to each other.

Our default setting is to respect!

Respect our father and mother, is of course, one of the ten commandments.

We are born with that respect in-built in us, but what happens to us thereafter causes us to disrespect others.

Two sayings I don't completely agree with are: "Respect your elders" and "You have to earn respect".

Respect your elders - of course we must but we should be respecting everyone regardless of their age. Just because I am older than someone doesn't mean I can demand respect if I don't respect that person as well.

Like trust, respect is a two-way street - I cannot respect someone who doesn't respect me.

The difficulty with that is, what if your father doesn't respect you?

Surely the ten commandments take precedent and this is one of the reasons why people end up with mental illnesses.

Parents can treat you without respect through abuse, both emotionally and physically.

So you have to respect them even though they may cause you long term harm!

You have to earn respect? No!

Our default setting should be to respect others unless they disrespect you.

There are no grey areas with respect.

How do you <u>earn</u> respect anyway?

Is there a certain point you get in a relationship which you reach, when you get told, "Well done! You have achieved your respect goal!"

What rubbish!

And you can't say," If that person respects me then I will respect them," - who are you to be the one who decides that?

Just because your boss is the boss, doesn't mean you must respect him if he always disrespects you.

Your job shouldn't demand that you respect your superiors regardless of how they treat you.

It's a human relationship which works both ways.

Once you lose respect it is extremely difficult, almost impossible to get that respect back.

There is too much water under the bridge.

People lost respect for me, for the crime I committed.

That is fine but most of them haven't found out from me personally, what transpired.

Respect is a personal choice and is yours only and should not be influenced by others.

Somebody else's loss of respect is not your baby.

*Loss of respect is what personally happens to you, and it should be something that person has done to **you** and not what they have done to someone else.*

Respect in prison is all over the place!

You are not respected for who you are, but the position you hold in the gang hierarchy.

Lower people are not respected and are treated like animals and end up sleeping on the floor.

Even though I was respected to a degree it didn't stop people from disrespecting my property.

And also it is disrespecting to continually ask someone for something - I was told that it costs nothing to ask, but that's not true, it costs you a loss of respect.

What makes it even worse is that the people asking for stuff from you were the ones smoking drugs all day.

They could afford drugs but had to beg for necessities.

I know what that feels like - your addiction prioritizes your needs, first your drug and then your living necessities.

In prison discipline is drilled into you and your fellow prisoners but it should start with respect because if you have respect you will have discipline.

Unfortunately in the gangs there will never be true respect as you are forced to respect someone because of his rank.

I applied my approach to respect to others and was successful with some but I was taken for a ride by others - but isn't that what happens in the real world?

I'm sure you have encountered it, I definitely have!

"If your goals are good then you will be respected, but if you are looking for trouble, that is what you will get."

Proverbs 11:27

Cancer

It was Easter 2015 and we went to visit my mom in Cape Town.

My mom had been battling with the left hand side of her body.

The left side of her face had dropped and she had limited use of her left hand and foot.

She was left-handed so that created a functional problem for her.

She had been to a couple of doctors who had diagnosed her with bell's palsy without bothering to do proper brain scans and tests.

We decided to get another opinion as her condition was deteriorating.

They did scans and x-rays at a hospital.

I was with her when she was told she had a brain tumor and it had spread to her lung.

It was devastating.

The surgeons at that hospital refused to operate on her, as my mom's medical aid would not cover it.

So we made alternative plans.

For me that was the commencement of a year long journey of seeing a happy, loving mother deteriorate to skin and bones, who couldn't even talk.

I lived 800km's away so I often had to make the journey on my own, and with my fear of flying, driving was the only realistic alternative.

The journey was obviously to visit her but also to see specialists and decide with my siblings what the best way forward was.

Everyone had their own opinion so that was not always an easy thing to decide!

When she passed away in March 2016, my oil level in my pot was close to full.

The stress, anxiety, depression was getting worse and worse, and her death came at the wrong time for me.

My mom had led a hard life, being emotionally and physically abused by my dad and then raising five children all with their own problems. She worked hard at looking after us all and when my dad died she had to fend for herself for 24 years. She had to get a job and that became a problem when she got too old. But she made plans baking her amazing cakes and her famous lemon meringue tarts and selling them to coffee shops.

Before she died she was finally happy in life, spending hours dancing and socializing, baking and cooking and visiting her 14 grandchildren.

Her death affected me more than I knew at the time.

I protected my feelings.

For example, at her memorial service I told humorous anecdotes about her and thereby avoiding the main issue.

After her death I was struggling to cope mentally.

Driving became an issue for me as I would have panic attacks whilst driving.

Sometimes I had to stop driving and pull over, in fear of an accident.

At one stage I had a bottle of vodka in the cubby hole to use to calm the huge stress.

I had to get it sorted out and this was the time I went onto anti stress tablets and then anti anxiety and depression tablets. Did they help?

They helped only in numbing my feelings i.o.w giving me a "I don't care" attitude to everything.

The oil in the pot was starting to boil over.

I was on a slippery slope and couldn't stop myself.

My gambling picked up around this time.

Sports betting at one stage became my passion and I uses to watch a lot of different sports because I would bet on a lot of sports.

Watching games became more exciting and with sports betting you could bet on anything happening in the game, for example, when the next goal was going to be scored or how many runs a batter would score.

It was still fun back then but in later years it became more intense.

At around about the same time, Stiffler introduced me a colleague of his, "coachy".

Now coachy was a regular gambler and a student of roulette systems.

He was busy on a roulette system which he said was unbeatable and if you had <u>discipline</u> you could make a nice income.

These systems were played on machines which have the same programming as slot machines.

So the payouts are regulated so I must stress, no system in the world can beat it.

But I got addicted to it very quickly - it was a combination of my love of numbers, it was a challenge and slot machines are highly addictive.

In the beginning it was fun but in later years became hell.........

———————

Problems encountered in prison
Reading Material

*Our constitution as per section 35(e) for detained and sentenced inmates, says that we have a right to conditions of sentence that are consistent with human dignity including at least exercise and the provision at state expense of amongst other necessities, **reading material.***

There is no reading material provided for detainees.

Absolutely bugger all.

I got lots and lots of books & magazines bought in via visits.

These were mostly lent, mostly on a permanent basis, to other inmates.

And the reading material had a positive affect on them.

I could see that they were less stressed, more subdued and happier.

Getting lost in a novel takes you away for a while from the hell of prison.

You get so lost in the story that you forget your own story and the story of others around you.

It helped me as well especially in solitary confinement.

The inmates didn't look after the books and some books were even used to smoke tobacco with - in fact some of them used pages of the Bible to smoke, what a sacrilege!!!

The State should refund me for all the books, that's for sure.

In maximum, I haven't as yet, seen any reading material.

What I do know is that my newspaper and magazine that came in on one of my visits, were sent back home. Not sure of the reason. Maybe they can be used as a weapon?

All I know is that I get to the read the Bible only and that is mine!

<u>*Pests and pest control*</u>

When you get to my age, you are sure you have encountered all the nasty insects in the world.

Think again!

The visible pests such as cockroaches, flies and spiders were plenty in the trial section but these visible insects you can live with.

It's the bed bugs or aka lice or aka twalas, that cause you to lose your sanity.

These are blood sucking insects ranging in size from a match head to a toenail.

They are nasty insects.

They hide in the seams of your clothing, intertwining themselves in the thread of your shirt, pants and underwear.

When you clean your clothing they don't die.

They even get into your shoes and slipslops.

At any time you could have thirty of these infidels on your body and you scratch non-stop.

You look around at the people in your cell and they all sit with their shirts off, examining the shirts closely, looking for the bloodsuckers!

When they bite it's equivalent to a bee sting.

And when you catch one and squash it between your fingernails, blood sprays out of their bodies.

They drove me mad.

Washing my body didn't help, washing my clothes didn't help.

The only way to get rid of them was to examine your clothing until you found them and then you had to find the parents!

There was talk that in years gone by pest control services were used, and we requested it from the supervisor a few times, but nothing of the sort ever happened.

Bugger all!

<u>Water problems</u>

Where do I start with the endless water problems?

In trial the water in the cell was to provide for 70 people for a myriad of reasons:

- *showering (you have the right to have a hot shower weekly)*
- *washing your face*
- *brushing your teeth*
- *washing your clothes*
- *drinking*
- *flushing the toilet (there is no flushing mechanism)*

This is good and well if there is a consistent water supply.

Our region was in a drought area and for a long time the water restrictions were present, but we still had sufficient water to do the things above.

*Every now and again you could have a **cold** shower.*

By the time you got to shower the hot water was finished.

Around September, after water restrictions were lifted as the dam levels were high enough, we ran into serious water problems in the cell.

The water was switched off for days, sometimes 10 days in a row.

We were told that the water pipes were broken in the area but the rumours were that the prison owed the municipality money - ie the State owed the State money, huh?

So as a result water was delivered to our cell in 25 litre drums, 100 litres for 70 people - that's 1.5 litres per person, for all the things above.

Clearly hopelessly too little.

So you prioritize and leave out washing and use it as mainly for drinking water.

Then for two days we didn't get any water.

I'm not sure why but for those two days you couldn't go to the toilet for a number two, as the toilet was overflowing.

One guy was so desperate that he went in the shower and then didn't have water to clean it!!!

Reasons were never given to us but the rumours we heard was that it was for punishment.

After that the gangs decided to strike as that was the only way the problem could get sorted out and it worked. Thereafter we got 200 litres for 70 people.

When the water came back on, it was only in the early mornings and early evenings like between 6 an 9 each day.

It was like it was planned and this continued in the maximum section.

I would estimate that in 14 months I have had about 10 hot showers.

I did not have one hot shower in single cells as the geyser was broken.

Water is life

St Albans is death

<u>*Noise in the cell*</u>

As mentioned before culture differences are extremely difficult to live with.

I prefer to live with very little noise as my wife can testify to.

That is why single cells suited me.

I don't mind noise during the daytime but before 6 in the morning and after 10 at night, there should be silence.

And some people stand next to each other and shout at the top of their voices.

The more excited they get, the louder they shout and there is nowhere to run to and escape the noise.

You are trapped like a caged animal.

Never mind the loud music!

I had a few verbal fights in the cells I was in, and the majority of the fights was due to somebody or somebodies waking me up at an obscene hour, with some loud noise.

Where is the discipline?

———————-

<u>*Racism, discrimination and Xenophobia*</u>

We have a long, well known history of racism and discrimination in this country.

In prison it's not just racism of Black vs White, but also Blacks vs Coloureds, Indian, Chinese.

It's always shown up in the words people use and it comes from all sources, prison wardens, est, gang members.

Discrimination against "mad" or different people is rife.

You are labeled if you are not the same as everyone else.

I was either called an mlungu, a boer, whitey, homeboy?

Names for mad people were "die-dies" or "cylons".

And if you came from another African country then you were considered an outcast.

They have no standing in prison.

They have money so they always have stuff so they are prime targets for thieves.

There is a definite hatred for a person of another colour, local or foreigner.

I had to listen to culturally different TV and radio programs and loud music but I never complained.

I think if the shoe was on the other foot there would have been lots of complaints!

<u>*Games day*</u>

On the last day of 2023 I organized a games day for the cell.

It consisted of "stokes" (prison ludo), crazy eights a card game and draughts.

I put up a prize to the value of R100 split between 1st, 2nd and 3rd.

About 32 people took part and they had great fun.

The dynamics in the cell shifted that day as they were all focused on the game and not on their stresses.

It took the whole day and finished at 18h00.

I didn't expect any thanks for what I did and I never got any, just complaints!

It was like my business career all over again! LOL

Seeing them happy for a day reminds me of the hour in the afternoon called "happy hour".

It was the time when we got food and this made everyone happy.

After everyone ate, the music went on and out came the tobacco, cigarettes and Marijuana and everyone was happy for a while!

Reckless years

In October 2016 we went on a golf tour to Thailand, paid for by our fundraising events.

The medication I was on helped me but my solution to flying was drinking as much alcohol as possible.

Alcohol was starting to become my crutch and an unhealthy solution to decreasing stress.

I managed to de-stress on that trip, mainly due to the help of Alcohol.

I got back with my oil levels a bit lower.

Alcohol and drugs were short term solutions to the problem though.

2016 to 2020 were reckless years for me.

I was trying every means possible to reduce the stress, but at work the stress was increasing, never decreasing.

The anti-anxiety drugs were not helping with the stress levels although my anxiety levels decreased.

I tried everything in those years to decrease the stress:

- walking
- golf
- alcohol
- cigarettes
- Marijuana
- long Friday lunches

But the main escape for me was gambling.

It eventually became a daily occurrence and the casino didn't help my addiction - they drowned me in alcohol and rewards such as hotel stays, meals, gifts, lucky draws and entertainment events.

It became a life within a life.

My work started to suffer and I started losing clients and I ended up in major debt.

Banks would phone me offering me large credit facilities, which obviously any gambling addict would grab with both hands!

It's like giving free drugs to a drug addict.

It can only make him worse.

Yes I was a gambling addict then but only one out of ten addicts seek help.

It's no wonder a large number of full blown gambling addicts commit suicide because full blown addiction is not fun, it is <u>hell</u>.

My gambling became worse and worse and much more intense - like my life depended on it.

The roulette machines took over my life.

I would win on a system for a while and then as soon as I lost I would change the system.

And my losses would be ten times more than my wins.

Here is an example of a day in my gambling life:

I would go either in the morning before work or afterwards once I had seen all my clients.

So like on a Tuesday, I would go to the casino at 7 in the morning, win within an hour (a set target amount like R1000), and then go to work.

That was the idea.

But it didn't always work out that way.

I would get there at 7 hoping to be out of there by 8, as I had lots of work to do.

My limit on my card was R8000 and then I could get another R3000 from money sent to my number.

So I would draw R3000 as my stake and stop-loss.

I would battle with the system and lose the R3000 and when I looked at the time, it would be after 9.

Now the stress would kick in as I had lost, but my addiction would not let me stop so I would let my client know that I wouldn't be coming in.

My next client was at 13h00 so I had more time now, so I went to draw R3000 and settled down for the next few hours to win back the initial R3000.

I switched my phone off as I could see messages coming through via whatsapp, email and missed phonecalls - but those could wait.

The next few hours I gradually lost the next R3000 and before long I was R6000 down.

The time was 12h30 and I had to go but I couldn't.

You reading this and thinking, just get up and leave, but an addict can't.

I phoned my next client and postponed my appointment to later on the week.

I drew the last R2000 of my limit.

I was stressed so I ordered a cider to take the edge off.

Now alcohol normally helped me when I gambled as I was less conservative.

So the afternoon I spent fighting my way back and having plenty of "soft" alcohol drinks.

By 4 o'clock I was at least R20000 up, over and above my original stake.

A good day at the office, however....

I couldn't leave as I couldn't go to work and I couldn't go home yet - I was expected home only at six.

My belief was that when you had a run of good luck you needed to may it worthwhile.

So I carried on and things started turning for the worse.

At 17h30 my money was gone and I was well on my way to being drunk.

I ordered a double whiskey and went to get my last R3000 which I could send to my phone number.

Now I would panic bet and throw money away to win the R11000 back and of course I lost.

Driving home I would tear up my casino card and throw it out the window vowing never to return.

At home I would continue drinking and check my phones and there would be lots of messages and emails requesting information from me - so effectively I was now a day behind in my work.

The next morning at work I would start working on a new system and as soon as I could I would be back at the casino, getting a new card and starting trying the new system.

This happened a lot.

I needed help then already.

Soon I gave up on the roulette machines and moved into the smoking section of the prive.

I started playing even more addictive slot machines, ones with flashing lights and nice music.

These machines put you in a trance-like state.

They mess with your mind.

You play so much for free spins and when you get them you win nothing.

But it pulls you in.

You start on a low bet but soon you are betting maximum as you want the thrill to get better.

It's a sick place to be in.

By March 2020 my pot was full of oil and any major trauma would cause devastation.

My luck would have it, that the covid19 pandemic reared it's ugly head.

The greatest pandemic the world has seen for centuries and deaths that hadn't been seen since World War 2.

So there I was in the middle of a pandemic, no money, no income for the foreseeable future, staff that depended on me, and uncontrollable stress levels.

The pot had to overflow and it did, in a massive devastating way!

The problem with the pandemic was that everything was locked down including physical casino establishments, but I had to find someway to escape.

I tried online gambling with what was left of my own credit, experimenting and testing my fathers horse racing systems.

One day in July 2020 the oil caught fire and the house started burning down.

I was drinking heavy alcohol at the time, either neat Tequila or mixed strong vodka drinks.

It helped drown my sorrows.

That caused me to make a mistake and "lend" R100,000 from one of the victim's business. It was **one** mistake that created a downward spiral. Like the start of a fire it only needed a spark.

In my disillusioned, distressed mind I thought I could solve my problems.

How you think in that situation is:

- <u>irrational</u> - it's behavior not associated with a rational logical person like myself;

- <u>illogical</u> - for a logical person like myself what I did made no logical sense. You don't win in gambling in fact if I measure my win % it was as low as 40%;

- <u>impulsive</u> - most gamblers are impulsive. If I saw a new game with big jackpots I would try it. If it required a big bet, I would do it;

- <u>desperate</u> - you become more and more desperate the more you gamble. You know you need to repay the money so you take more desperate risks;

- <u>delusional</u> - thoughts like the victims won't mind, they owe me money, they have enough money etc enter your head. The thing is in that state there is no ways I could stop the thoughts - they were overriding and overpowering.

- <u>obsessive</u> - It became my every thought, my only priority and everything else suffered, my family, my friends, my staff, my work, God - it takes control and it doesn't let go. If you know of an obsessive person or you are one, then you know what happens to you. I've see Ironmen become obsessed with the sport to a point where it takes over their lives and it becomes their priority, just like this.

My problems were not solved but were exacerbated 100 fold.

Everyone presumes I had millions lying in my bank - the 100% fact is that I never had a cent. The money would come in, get transferred to the online gambling platforms leaving me with nothing. If I won, the balance would get transferred out daily and repaid immediately to the victims, leaving me with nil.

So who gained out of this crime?

The gambling companies and the State.

I was used to dealing with millions every day of my life for 22 years, so R100,000 wasn't a lot of money and online gambling takes away the "money" feel - its just credits.

1000 credits is R1000 but it doesn't feel the same as if you take notes and fed R1000 into a machine.

It shows you what state of mind I was in when I never even kept record of the money I was taking, and I am an accountant who keeps records for a living.

My mindset was such that the winnings paid the victims back, so my debt was settled - if one of the victims or their staff came to me at any time and said I owed millions maybe that would have put out the fire, but nobody bothered.

I didn't even mean to take from the other victim.

All the bank accounts appeared on one online banking profile.

In my state of mind I never knew what I was doing and that's why it is a mental illness.

I was on automation.

I had imploded.

The house was burning down.

————————-

Mental illness in prison is plentiful.

I would go as far to say that it is the cause of the majority of crimes and most of the illnesses can be fixed with medication or therapy.

I good example is a friend I had in my cell who without doubt had ADHD.

I would be speaking to him and he would drift off for a while, like he had noticed something more interesting and then when I called him he would snap back into reality.

I'm not an expert in this field, but when I asked him questions his answers fitted into the mould of an ADHD person, which my wife, the teacher, had described to me in great detail.

His crime was violence at home.

This was due to the ADHD and was exacerbated with the use of crystal meths.

I would think drugs or alcohol would make the illness worse.

When I suggested that he go and sees a phychologist, he was horrified, like I had just suggested he run around the cell naked!

So the State should screen detainees/convicts and come up with an easy solution to the problem - this is how you sort out crime through proactive individualized solutions.

If my mate was on Ritilin he would not have ended up in prison twice!

He is out now and doing OK, as his mom sent him to church studies, but he still doesn't have work bland without that he could go back to crime.

But with ADHD it's difficult to become a good worker without the right medication.

Get to the root cause of the problem.

As I mentioned there are a lot of mental illnesses in prison.

Niekie is a good example, who I will write about below.

A lot of these people don't know what's wrong with them and how to fix it.

The State's current solution to the problem is to throw the really bad "die-die's" into their own special cell, so they can be managed differently.

So the poor wardens have to manage criminals and mentally ill people.

There was a newspaper headline recently in the local press, in April 2024, on that exact subject, "prison wardens are forced to look after mentally ill patients".

Basically the union was not happy with the wardens work conditions and their added responsibility of looking after mentally ill criminals.

The prison mental facilities belonging to the State are so full that you can wait a year before going there.

So what is the plan with mental offenders?

I have a mental illness but mine is treatable by abstinence and self-discipline.

That doesn't mean that I can manage on my own - that's what professionals are there for.

You are in the worst place in the world but you have no help for your mental health.

In the trial section of prison, mental health professionals are non-existent.

A guy in single cells told me that he had seen a social worker once in seven years - that's a social worker and not a phychologist - a big difference.

My crime was caused by a mental illness and with treatment and group therapy it's easy to fix.

I have seen a phychologist once in 14 months and that was April 2024.

It was not really any help as the phychologist is leaving prison soon and it would be worthless to start treatment.

Nevertheless, he did have some good advice and agreed that I should be appealing my sentence.

<u>Niekie</u>

There is so much to say about Niekie, so I will try to keep it short.

Niekie is a highly intelligent man, a Muslim, but he has several mental illnesses.

He told me he had bi-polar but he is also a drug addict.

In his body he had implants which he said were cameras, which are there to analyze his illnesses.

When I met him for the first time, it was in the communal cell, when I returned for the second time.

I knew nothing of him but I was soon to find out!

When you are in prison you are wary of everybody and it takes time to assess and understand who they are.

Within an hour of meeting him, I heard him shouting the worst obscenities to a guy in the cell.

He was calling the guy's mother names and the guy names, names like "kaffir" a name banned in South Africa.

I thought to myself, here comes BIG trouble.

But everyone else was laughing.

Someone had messed with Niekie's food and that was his standard reaction.

It was his default setting to swear at the instigator.

It didn't have the same effect as it was the way he always spoke.

He wasn't physically aggressive.

I don't think he would hurt a fly but he was most definitely verbally aggressive.

I had a love-hate relationship with him at first.

He would make me laugh and write the greatest letters to me - ones that would inspire me and others.

A lot of his writings were Muslim prayers, prayers of hope and peace.

A few days after he met me, he stole my box of smokes and my lighter.

He had a habit of crawling on the floor pretending he was cleaning and then would take what he could find - he was also a kleptomaniac.

I was angry as he stole my lighter - the number one prize possession in prison.

He never owned up to it and he refused to be searched.

The second time he stole from me, he stole a new packet of smokes from me which I had stashed in my bed.

He gave himself away though, as he was handing out cigarettes to everyone.

He was called to the stairs and forced to buy me a new packet - months later he apologized.

He came back to prison on three separate occasions during my year on trial.

All of his crimes were as a result of his mental illnesses - breaking things in his parents house, stealing things etc.

His drug habit was alarming!

He would get money everyday from his parents, who were quite well off.

He would tell them it was for food or toiletries or medicine, but it all went on drugs.

In one day he could smoke five Marijuana zols, a small packet of crystal meths and a tablet of mandrax, and then he was properly stoned!

Crystal meths keeps you awake and he would go days without sleeping and when he wasn't on drugs he was an angry beast!

The one time he approached me in the bathroom and asked me rudely for a cigarette. I refused and he became very aggressive with me - he came close to hitting me but I knew he wouldn't as it wasn't his nature and besides he liked me!

His conversations with his mom were sometimes the worst but that was when they didn't want to give him money.

Drugs was his main problem.

He had been to mental institutions plenty of times but with no good results.

He knew he was mentally ill but there was nothing he could do about it.

Despite our history we became good friends and he always came to visit me in single cells.

He was always on the hunt for something to eat but he always gave me stuff in return, a phenomenon in prison!

He brought me the best avocado ever!

He loved food and he was always fighting about food with the cooks and wardens.

I miss the guy and hopefully will see him again.

I still have his letters and here is an extract from one (translated from Afrikaans).

30 Jan 2024 from Niekie dedicated to Jonathan Blow:

"May Allah make your heart clean of spiteful feelings. I am writing this letter in all sincerity.

Many times in our life we go through difficult times and then we must try to accept the situation with patience. One thing I know is that God (Allah) will never desert you especially if you believe that Allah/God exists.

Jonathan I don't know you outside prison but the time I have known you in prison I can see that you are there to help me and I can truly say that I owe you a lot. But I really want to give you hope for the future. May the Allah give you the hope and I truly believe in the Almighty Allah. May the Almighty Allah protect you and you must know one thing that nothing can happen without the help of Allah.

May the Almighty Allah God save you and make you a free man forever after the prison sentence.

Never look at people that have more than you, rather look at people that have less than you. And then you will appreciate what you have!

<u>Empathy</u>

You need to walk in someone's shoes in order to fully understand their behavior.

It shows caring, love and respect for another human being.

Before we jump to conclusions find out the source of the bad behavior.

As a manager or leader in a business, empathy should be one of your tools of management.

It can solve problems before they escalate.

When I took bought the retail business in 2022 (that will be talked about in the next chapter), the staff's morale was down on *the ground. The reasons were mainly due to a lack of empathy from the previous owners.*

When you are managing lots of staff you need go find time to listen to their problems and then you will find out the reasons for their misbehavior.

All people have problems, no matter who you are and its sometimes it's very easy to solve those problems together.

We are born with empathy in us, it's our default setting and part of our human nature.

But humans stop caring about others for some reasons - maybe it's because they have too many problems themselves.

You have to be mentally strong and love yourself, in order to have empathy for others.

I have always had empathy and was a strong point of mine.

But empathy can drain you mentally and emotionally.

You take on board other people's problems.

As I was not strong enough, being empathetic had a negative affect on me.

I may have helped others but it made me worse.

Now it's completely different for me.

I am strong so empathy makes me stronger.

Helping people motivates me especially those less fortunate than me.

"Help to carry one another's burdens and in this way you will obey the Law of Christ. If someone thinks he is somebody when really he is a nobody, he is only deceiving himself. Each one should judge his own conduct, if it is good, then he can be proud of what he himself has done, without having to compare it with what someone else has done."

Corinthians 6:2

"He helps us in all our troubles, so that we are able to help others who have all kinds of trouble, using the same help that we ourselves have received from God".

2 Corinthians 1:4

Trying to make amends

July 2021 - I caught covid. I was not going to clients much as the third wave of covid had hit and it was a lot worse this time. I was going to clients for urgent matters only, as I could work from home.

One of the victims asked me to meet with his butchery consultant to discuss figures and gp's.

I met with him and the consultant was sick.

I should have left straight away but I felt obliged to do what the victim had asked me to do.

The consultant said he had flu!

Flu during covid, I don't think so.

So he was sneezing and coughing all over the place.

The next day he phoned me to say that he had covid.

He had made me and two office ladies sick as well.

I was sick as a dog for two weeks but luckily I had had the first vaccine jab, so I survived, but alas the consultant didn't.

RIP Malcolm.

In March 2022 after 3 months of negotiating, meetings and mountains of work, I bought a retail business with a partner.

My idea, and a lie detector will prove this, was to invest in a business for the victims to repay the debt I had made with them.

Feasibility studies showed that in 5 years time the victims could have R20m.

My now ex-partner in the business told me he had the capital to put down as a deposit for the business.

I was going to run the business with my knowledge and know-how.

My ex-partner had lied about the amount of money he had for a deposit and as a result we were R2m short.

So the deal was going to collapse and then the victims would never get their money back.

So I had to make a decision.

Which I did and took R2m of my winnings and paid for the shares instead of repaying the victims.

It was always my <u>intention</u> to build an asset for the victims.

In fact when my ex-partner kicked me out the business in Dec 2022, the value of my 50% was R3.5m, using the same valuation method I used to buy the business.

My ex-partner eventually wangled the shares for R1.8m as <u>he</u> had let the business deteriorate.

A year after I was kicked out the business by him, he was still blaming me for things going wrong.

The way he handled the whole saga shows you what type of person he is.

An arrogant, self-centred greedy person.

But I loved owning the business. It helped me and it lifted the staff's morale to new heights.

They are such good people and today I still get support from them, even though I am an outcast from society.

I miss them!

————————————-

Est (emergency support team) aka "taakmag" which loosely translated means powertask.

These guys are independent of the prison wardens and have a job to do, but sometimes it's the way you do the job that matters.

Section 14 of the Constitution says," <u>Everyone</u> has the right to privacy, which includes the right not to have: (a) their persons or their homes searched and (b) their property searched.

They are in a difficult position as they have to keep the prison safe and secure, free of drugs, weapons, phones and other illegal stuff. They technically should only be searching government property but they don't - they search you and all your private stuff.

My experience with them was not good.

For someone with anxiety and violence issues, it can be distressing.

They can come into your cell without warning, any time of the day or the night.

You never know when, and it's scary.

The first time I encountered them was at six am on a Sunday morning.

I was still in bed.

You hear loud stamping on the concrete floor, like a rumble of thunder, which reverberates throughout the cell walls, floors and cement ceiling.

They use a plastic key so you don't hear them coming in.

The next thing you hear is shouts of, "down, down, down!" And everyone dives to the floor.

You look up and see black clothed men with weapons standing next to you while you lie on the dirty concrete floor - yes you have to lie on the floor!

Next you walk out the cell with your hands held high, and if you don't walk fast enough they push you aggressively.

You are then made to sit with your hands on your head.

After that you are told to stand facing the wall with your hands above you planted on the dirty wall.

They do a thorough search of your body.

You are then taken back to your cell to fetch your mattress and your personal belongings.

You carry these outside, they are searched and all your clothes and bedding are thrown on the floor.

While this is happening the cell is being taken apart.

I mean literally **torn** *apart.*

Beds are taken apart, clothing is thrown all over, the makeshift curtains are torn and confiscated.

Once your stuff has been searched you get to sit, this time on your mattress and not the floor.

This is about the time when people who have lockers get called to go and unlock them.

The first couple of searches they didn't call anyone to unlock their lockers, they forced them open or cut them with bolt cutters.

You then go back to your cell and face a rubbish dump - beds upside down, paper and water on the floor, clothes strewn all over.

So as I said they were there to do their jobs but it's the way you do it.

The **<u>one</u>** *thing they cannot do, is touch you or hit you for no reason - I understand if you resist them or fight with them but I would never do that.*

The one time we were called to open our lockers. I followed their instructions.

Their commands came from different people - so one guy says "stand here" and you do that, and then another guy pushes you and says," go open your locker".

This happened and then someone said something racist about me, so I replied unagressively - then the one est guy hit me in the back with his baton and the other one kicked me in the shins, saying don't be clever whitey!

Yes they are racist, they called me whitey, boer, mlungu, spies (the white guy head of est).

All these names are racist as they define you by the colour of your skin, which I didn't choose, God gave to me.

The other thing they did was mess with my stuff in my locker.

The one time all my cigarettes were taken out their boxes and thrown on the floor, a lot of them getting wet and useless.

My two litre coke went missing and who knows what else.

They had a job to do, but it's the way you do it.

My letters to the head of prison spelt that out but there was no response!

————————-

<u>Prison wardens</u>

Servants of the State, these people are paid do a job.

Amongst their responsibilities are to ensure the safety and security of prisoners.

And to ensure meals, exercise, visits, shop, treatment, accommodation are all adequately given.

Basically they are here to make sure the prisoners get their rights as per the Constitution of South Africa.

But they don't do their jobs.

They sit around most of the time and when you ask them a question they either ignore you or tell you to ask another warden.

They don't control or run the prison.

The gangs do and that's why their priorities are not the prisoners but the gang leaders.

They fear the gangs and for good reason.

One command and they could lose their life.

90% of requests I asked the prison wardens - important things such as treatment, rules exercise were ignored but a gang leader could ask a petty question and they would jump.

In single cells, the big lady wardens who sat there "looking after us", did sweet nothing.

Everytime I saw them they were eating or drinking coffee.

What made it worse is that they had a prisoner cleaner who they would call all the time and most of the time it was to pass them something just out of their reach .

What a lovely job they had!

They get paid to sit around and do nothing and have a free servant to answer to their every beck and call.

Another thing these prison wardens like to do, is to ask you for food or cigarettes.

They use their position of power and abuse it.

Once I came back from a visit, hurrying to get back to the safety of my cell.

A police warden followed me, some guy I hadn't even seen before.

I got into my cell and took out some long awaited for KFC (fried chicken).

He appeared at my door and took a piece for himself.

You cannot argue or fight with them as these are the people who unlock your doors for you.....

———————————

Discovery

In Sept 2022, I gambled for the last time ever...

In Oct 2022, I went to Portugal. Now this trip was planned in Jan 2022 already and was planned by my golf club.

The golf club paid for my trip.

My wife, who is a teacher and has been for thirty years, had saved up some money and the rest I paid out of my income, so that her and the kids could join me for a week. Her parents also had to lend her R50k as there were flight problems.

The prosecutor insinuated that I had used the proceeds of my theft to pay for the trip, without checking the facts.

She had also told a story that I had stashed the money overseas in Portugal, a story she had got from my ex-partner.

I'm not sure why the story was made up as the proof of what happened to the money was there for all to see. In fact the victims and their lawyers got all of my bank statements in Dec 2022 which proved what happened to the funds.

In my opinion, false gossipers are evil and stupid, and you just have to read the Bible to back that statement up!

The Portugal trip was hugely stressful for me and I think I knew that the proverbial shit was about to hit the fan, when I returned back to South Africa.

In November 2022 discovery of the theft came to light.

I spent the next three months sorting out a settlement agreement which enabled the victims to get my shares of the retail shop.

I also went to a phychologist to sort out my chronic addiction and got mechanisms of how to prevent relapses.

I was also trying to find alternative employment as both my businesses were not mine any longer.

I took full responsibility for what I did, that is stated on record in court.

The thing is, there were other parties who were responsible and other parties who benefitted from this crime.

The victims and their employees should have queried the amounts going into my business bank account.

Nothing was hidden, the bank account was not changed and was the same account I paid my monthly retainer into.

If one of them had asked me the question, I would have told the truth, I know that - I can't lie if asked a direct question.

The crime would have been stopped in the early days.

The bank employees should also have picked up the payments and queried it.

I apparently was like "family" to the victims.

They both said so in court.

A scripted question and answer session.

There is a lot I can write about what they said but the important thing to me is what they said about me being like "family".

- Family spend a lot of time together
- I saw the victims only in work environments.
- This was for two days a week
- Family is a two way relationship
- I knew about their lives and problems.
- What did they know about me?
- Family spend important days together
- I invited them to my 40th & 50th birthdays
- They came to my 40th but declined my 50th

- I was never invited to their birthdays.

• Families go on holiday together, kids and all

- One weekend in 18 years

• Families know everything about each other

- They did not know I gambled regularly

So I was not family of theirs.

I was a consultant and someone they could use and abuse.

But when it was convenient to them, I was family!

The parties that benefitted from the crime, were the gambling companies and the State.

The gambling companies knew how much I was spending but not once, I repeat **not once**, did they ask me where all the money was coming from or proof thereof.

They also didn't give me any addiction help lines or phone me to check if I was addicted.

They closed my account as soon as I asked these questions.

The State set the regulations for these gambling companies and guess what? They earned 28% of the gambling income - about R8m in my case.

They have no motivation to change the regulations as it's good income for them.

But people get hurt badly by the online gambling companies - they lose all their money, lose family and friends and sometimes commit suicide.....

On 16th March 2023 I was arrested for theft of R28m, which is equivalent to $1.5m or £1.2m.

After my arrest my <u>stress</u> disappeared, lifting a huge weight off my shoulders.

I was like a new person.

I could think clearly and make rational decisions again.

My default setting had been reset.

Let's talk about my sentence.

I never had a trial as I pleaded guilty when asked the question in court.

In most countries this would mean a huge reduction in my sentence, but not in my case.

Apart from that factor I had plenty of mitigating factors which were not taken into account or were spoken about by my lawyer (I had sent her all the factors to talk about).

The more money you steal, the harsher the sentence.

I stole R28m as a result of a mental illness.

If someone steals R100 from you and they repay you back R40, then they have stolen R60.

R60 is the amount you have permanently lost.

Theft is defined as taking something that does not belong to you, on a permanent basis **but** what if that something is returned to you?

Especially if they are "family".

So let's call a spade a spade.

The theft amount was R28m.

The other important point when it comes to the amount involved is that an addict will fuel his addiction for as long as he can - **especially** a gambler who does not get sick or die from his addiction like an alcoholic or drug addict.

Talking about drug addicts, two drug dealers were sentenced on 6 October 2023 for a R400m cocaine bust. The one got 10 years and the other 3 years. Drugs they were going to sell to thousands of drug users and thereby affecting thousands of lives.

Here are some examples of people who stole more money than me and they all had the mental illness, gambling disorder:

- Andrew Caspersen (USA) stole R760m and got 4 years;
- Michael D'Allessio (USA) stole R1160m and got 6 years;
- Martin Sargeant (UK) stole R100m and got 5 years;
- Aphrodite Myron (Aus) stole R38m and got 49 months;
- Julien Kremer (UK) stole R45m and got 5 years;
- Donna Wozniak (USA) stole R80m and got 6 years.

These people all suffered from gambling addiction/gambling disorder/pathological gambling.

In fact the highest sentence I have seen in the world was Cody Easterday who stole R4billion and he got 11 years.

I got 22 years.

On top of that I lost my CA qualification which is an effective 3 year punishment, as that is how long it took me to get it.

- Jonathan Blow (SA) stole R28m and got 25 years!!!!

Suffering

YOU THINK YOU HAVE IT BAD.

Jesus died on the cross to save us.

Paul in 2 Corinthians 11:16-33 spoke of his suffering:-

- *he went to prison many times;*
- *he was whipped much more than his prison time;*
- *on five occasions he was whipped 39 lashes by the Jews;*
- *on three occasions he was whipped by the Romans;*
- *once he was stoned;*
- *three times he was in shipwrecks;*
- *he was in the water for 24 hours;*

- *he was in danger from floods;*
- *he was in danger from robbers;*
- *he was in danger from fellow Jews;*
- *he was in danger from Gentiles;*
- *he was in danger in the cities, in the wild, on the high Seas and from false friends;*
- *he went often without sleep;*
- *he went hungry and thirsty;*
- *he was often without food, shelter or clothing;*
- *he was under daily pressure from churches.*

Acts 9:15-16 says this about Saul (before his name changed to Paul):

"The Lord said to him, **"Go, because I have chosen him (Paul) to serve me, to make my name known to Gentiles and Kings and the people of Israel, and I myself will show him all that he must suffer for my sake."**

God's promises come true!

An addict's allegory

I owned a Boeing Business Jet, a plane that could hold up to fifty passengers and crew.

The aeroplane was my business, the passengers were my clients and the crew was my few staff members.

I flew and maintained the plane myself, and together with my crew, ensured the passengers were happy, comfortable and got to their destination safely.

I ran the business by myself, and together with my staff ensured that the clients were happy and their goals were achieved.

Twenty years ago I started flying for a few interested customers, and through good service and reliability, my customer base increased.

Through my good service and reliability, word of mouth increased my client base exponentially.

The increase in customers prevented me from ensuring the plane was in tip top shape - wear and tear took it's toll over the years, and all I was doing was patching up the problems instead of buying new parts.

The growth in my client base prevented me from looking after my own business, as my focus was on those who needed my help. My business problems were continually patched up and not fixed on a permanent basis.

You see the customers kept me busy, 24/7.

I did get some help over the years but that help was unreliable, and some customers stopped flying with me due to the bad service delivered by my help.

I brought in top people to help me but they left due to better offers or incompetence. You see, it was not easy to work for these clients - they were demanding and not appreciative of a lot of after hours work that had to be done.

A small minority of the customers would thank me each time we landed safely, but the majority couldn't care less - they were focused on themselves and their greed.

I flew through storms and turbulence, but not once did the passengers say, "We Trust you, Mr. Pilot, to get us to our destination safely."

It was taken for granted and not once did any of them ask if I needed help in any way, to make sure the plane would survive for the long term.

I was never asked if I needed help with my business and never once did I hear the words, "I trust you". During very difficult times I helped clients get out of financial trouble, and their businesses reached new heights with my involvement.

So I battled through the years and my record was outstanding.

I built the clients wealth, making them millions of Rands in personal wealth.

Happy customers left me during this period having accomplished their goals, but still no appreciation was shown towards my dedication, loyalty, love and care.

These clients left having achieved their personal wealth goals. It was because of me that their businesses were sold for good prices.

One day, on route to our destination, the worst storm that has been seen on earth for centuries appeared out of nowhere.

The storm was covid19, the worst pandemic to hit the earth in centuries.

Blinding torrential rain, hurricane winds, thunder and lightning came down - the plane was getting hit from all sides.

It came at the wrong time for my business - my business was not strong enough. It was a devastating pandemic wiping out millions of people and businesses. I was in trouble.

I was trying to remain calm and was focused on getting the plane safely to it's destination.

The majority of the passengers were carrying on, unaware of the problems I was facing.

There were some who should have known what was happening.

Two clients were supposed to have realised the problem. Them or their staff should have been more vigilant.

There were some who were sick from the storm.

Even though I was having personal turmoil, I still showed my care for the sick clients and prayed for them daily.

There were some who expressed their concerns, but not loud enough.

I had also lost radio contact in the storm - I was trying to talk but nothing was happening.

I could hear voices but couldn't make out what they were saying.

I couldn't talk to anyone - addict's don't. Only one out of every 10 addict's talk to professionals about their addiction. I couldn't even listen to advice, my mind had gone into another world.

Suddenly the plane's engine and instruments stopped working, the system was in complete and utter failure.

I lost control, completely and utterly. It was the loss of control that caused me to make <u>one</u> bad decision, that caused massive devastation.

I lost total control of flying the plane - it was out of my hands.

The plane was hurtling towards earth on a collision course with the ground below.

Some passengers shouted in their drunken state, "DON'T WORRY WE TRUST YOU MR PILOT, YOU HAVE NEVER LET US DOWN BEFORE!"

But I didn't know what to do.

This was a totally new situation for me and the plane was in freefall.

The clients were unawares of my calamity, but they still trusted me, a broken person.

I tried everything to fix the problem, and every now and again the plane would correct itself back to stability, but that didn't last long.

Every now and again during the 2 year freefall, I righted the ship for a brief period, but once you lose control you are doomed.

I was in shock.

I couldn't even warn the passengers of our impending doom and a crash landing.

I couldn't even warn clients what was happening to me.

There was no stopping the crash.

I managed to steer the plane onto a landing area but the rest was in God's hands.

God looked after the passengers - all of them surviving.

A few injured but not too seriously.

Two of the clients were damaged but the rest of the clients were untouched by my downfall.

Unfortunately I didn't survive - the pilot died in the crash, never to fly again.

The downfall took me and my business out for good.

Some of the passengers were happy I was gone.

Some couldn't care less.

A few were sad..

That's what happens to an addict...... YOU CRASH AND BURN.

Not one client came to my funeral.

Isn't THAT sad.

Learnings

I have learnt a lot from this experience and writing this book.

It's important for me to highlight some learnings so that maybe this kind of catastrophic event won't happen to you or someone you know.

1. *__Addiction__*

This is what caused my crime.

It's amazing how an addict can keep things secret for such a long time and as mentioned it's very seldom that an addict seeks help.

__But__ *in hindsight there are certain signs you can pick up on:*

- *secretive nature - the person is secretive about his phone, tablet, laptop. He keeps these things private. His personal and business finances are also kept private;*
- *anti-social behavior - declining events, family gatherings, parties. Not answering his phone is a dead give away;*
- *drinking alcohol at strange times of the day;*
- *irritable reactions to normal occurrences;*
- *not looking after himself - appearance, health, mental state.*

2. *__Stress__*

Addiction was the cause but I think stress was the root of the cause. Stress stemming from childhood and gradually getting worse until it caused the catastrophic event.

Here are some learnings to help with stress:

- *Face every test on its own merits. Do not worry about tomorrow as that has its own stresses;*
- *Spend some time planning. I find a Sunday night is a good time to plan for the week;*

- *Expect the unexpected. It will help you remain calmer.*
- *Take vacations that will reduce your stress levels. If you hate flying then don't fly!*
- *Exercise and sport will give your stress a rest;*
- *Have a set routine - prison has helped me in that regard. Everyday you should have a set routine so that if something unexpected happens you can deal with it;*
- *Communicate with those people that stress you out. Their stress can cause you stress. I failed to deal with those kinds of people, they would attack me with their issues as soon as I walked in the door!*
- *Deal with your to do list. Don't bury your head in the sand;*
- *Good sleep is important. If you feel tired then sleep, you are not going to miss anything important!*
- *Do **not** turn to unhealthy ways of dealing with stress. A sober person is able to deal with stress a lot easier!*

3. ***Love***

It's important for functional families to talk about love so that you grow up knowing about the most important thing in life and in the Bible.

- *Tell your children and friends that you love them;*
- *You have to love yourself. You have to change to love yourself first.*
- *Loving yourself means working on your body, mind and spirit;*
- *Support and love your family and friends unconditionally, no matter what happens to them. Especially someone with a mental illness;*
- *Love the Lord with all your heart, soul, mind and strength.*

4. ***Respect***

Respect is something we grew up with but unfortunately it has lost some of its meaning. Kids nowadays don't respect their parents. There was numerous crimes which I heard about while on trial, to do with kids abusing their parents in some way.

- *Respect your mother and father regardless;*
- *Respect all people unless you have a very good reason not to;*
- *A position of power does not mean you get to demand respect!*

5. <u>**Judging**</u>

I feel my experience has taught me plenty about judging.

It takes something bad to happen to really get the true opinion of people.

Hearing one side of a story is not good enough.

*Reading a news article, which must be the truth, only gives you one side of a story <u>**unless**</u> the person targeted is also interviewed or had his say.*

- *Judges and magistrates are put in positions to judge you here on earth. Accept that.*
- *If you are perfect then you can judge others;*
- *Look at the good things the person did and not just the one bad thing.*

6. <u>**Some other learnings**</u>

- *Your mindset does not have to be the same as those around you - whatever your situation is. Stick to your own morals and principles;*
- *Make sure your family is a functional family. There are lots of books on this topic;*
- *I can't stress this enough, but tell the **truth** at all times. Even if it gets you into trouble. God does not like liars.*
- *Family is a two way relationship.*

Most importantly if you feel something is not right in your life or someone else's then DO SOMETHING ABOUT IT!

If ever you want to ask me a question or make a comment or just chat you can reach me on:

Email: jossblow5677@gmail.com

X: @ Johnny478241002

Instagram: Johnny Martin

Facebook: Johnny Simon

www.ingramcontent.com/pod-product-compliance
Lightning Source LLC
Chambersburg PA
CBHW052034150726
48002CB00002B/594